BUSY MOM'S GUIDE

to Parenting Teens

Busy Mom's
GUIDE

to Parenting Teens

PAUL C. REISSER, M.D.

Tyndale House Publishers, Inc.
Carol Stream, Illinois

THE OFFICIAL BOOK OF

THE
FOCUS ON
THE FAMILY
PHYSICIANS RESOURCE
COUNCIL, U.S.A.

Visit Tyndale online at www.tyndale.com.

Visit Focus on the Family at www.FocusOnTheFamily.com.

TYNDALE and Tyndale's quill logo are registered trademarks of Tyndale House Publishers, Inc.

Focus on the Family and the accompanying logo and design are federally registered trademarks of Focus on the Family, Colorado Springs, CO 80995.

Busy Mom's Guide to Parenting Teens

Copyright © 2012 by Focus on the Family. All rights reserved. Edited by Linda Washington; produced with the assistance of The Livingstone Corporation.

Adapted from the *Complete Guide to Baby and Child Care*, ISBN 978-1-4143-1305-4. Copyright © 2007 by Focus on the Family.

Cover photograph copyright © Fancy/Photolibrary. All rights reserved.

Designed by Jennifer Ghionzoli

Library of Congress Cataloging-in-Publication Data

Reisser, Paul C.
   Busy mom's guide to parenting teens / Paul C. Reisser.
      p. cm.
   "Adapted from the Complete guide to baby and child care"—T.p. verso
   Includes bibliographical references (p.   ) and index.
   ISBN 978-1-4143-6461-2 (sc)
1. Motherhood—Religious aspects—Christianity. 2. Parent and teenager—Religious aspects—Christianity. 3. Parenting—Religious aspects—Christianity. 4. Child rearing—Religious aspects—Christianity. I. Title.
   BV4529.18.R455 2012
   649´.125—dc23
                                                              2012000821

Printed in the United States of America

18 17 16 15 14 13 12
7   6   5   4   3   2   1

●●● CONTENTS

●●●FOREWORD

FIFTY YEARS AGO popular visions of the "world of tomorrow" included not only flying cars and routine trips to outer space, but also twenty- to thirty-hour workweeks and a bounty of leisure time for everyone by the end of the twentieth century.

Instead, more than a decade into the twenty-first century, we are dealing with exponential increases in the complexity of our lives. We're working harder than ever to earn a living while juggling family responsibilities and a multitude of other commitments. Even when we're supposedly "off duty," there are always dozens of e-mails to wade through, cell phones sounding off at all hours, and social networking sites beckoning night and day. Furthermore, if we need information about anything, Google will be happy to summon more websites than we can possibly visit. Yet this overabundance of information sources doesn't always satisfy our need for wisdom and insight, especially when dealing with issues concerning some of the most important people in our lives: our teenage children.

For more than three decades Focus on the Family has been a trusted resource for mothers and fathers as they have navigated the entire journey of parenting, from the first baby's cry in the delivery room to the release of their last young adult to (hopefully) responsible independence. Several years ago Focus on the Family's Physicians Resource Council prepared the *Complete Guide to Baby and Child Care*, and in 2007 a revised and expanded edition of this book was released. I had the privilege of serving as the primary author for both editions and can say without hesitation that the book was definitely *complete*, weighing in on virtually every topic related to parenting and the health of infants, children, and teens. At nine hundred pages, this was not a book to tuck into a handbag for a casual read over lunch.

Teens never fail to give parents plenty to think about (or lose sleep over), and busy schedules aren't always compatible with the task of sifting through the good and bad parenting advice on the Internet, or wading through the contents of a large book. We thus thought it would be helpful to distill the *Complete Guide*'s core concepts about parenting teens into a smaller volume.

We have framed key ideas in the form of questions and answers, and have included a lot of practical advice, while trying to avoid a cookbook approach to parenting. Teenagers are not built like cars or computers; they do not come with instruction manuals that guarantee that *B* will happen if you do *A*. Furthermore, what may work like a charm for one teen may prove to be an utter failure with another. Nevertheless, parenting is too important a task to approach without spending some time studying a basic road map and reviewing some trustworthy traveler's advisories.

This book is one in a series of Busy Mom's Guides, all of which are intended to provide help and hope for important concerns of family life. By the way, we would be very pleased if these guides would prove useful to some busy dads as well.

Paul C. Reisser, M.D.
November 2011

●●●INTRODUCTION

Listen, my son, accept what I say,
  and the years of your life will be many.
I guide you in the way of wisdom
  and lead you along straight paths.

PROVERBS 4:10-11

BETWEEN THE TWELFTH and twenty-first birthdays, your child will undergo rapid and intense physical, psychological, and social changes, and at the end of this period he will no longer be a child. Just as you probably approached the "terrible twos" (sometimes called the first adolescence) with a combination of eager anticipation and a little apprehension, you may now have a similar mix of positive expectation and growing concern as the "real thing" arrives. Without a doubt, adjustments and challenges are ahead for everyone in the family.

Indeed, the years ahead may at times feel like a canoe trip down a mountain river. The scenery is constantly changing; the ride is always interesting and often pleasant; but choppy waters, roaring rapids, and an occasional waterfall may await you around the next bend. Your job will be to stabilize the family canoe as much as possible and by all means prevent it from turning over before your adolescent reaches the calmer waters of adulthood.

It won't all be trials and turbulence. These are highly rewarding years for many families, full of accomplishments, commitments to worthwhile causes, and experiences that weren't possible when your child was younger. You can't expect your two-year-old to appreciate a basketball game, a performance of your favorite stage production, or a great sermon, but your sixteen-year-old can share these experiences with you and be as interested or enthralled as any adult.

This book will begin with a look at the physical aspects of this remarkable transformation from child to adult. Emotions, relationships, the desire for independence, and other growing pains will be discussed in the next chapter. In subsequent chapters we will address a number of areas of concern for parents and teens alike: the wise use of electronic media; sexuality; alcohol and drug abuse; bullying; eating disorders; and depression. We will conclude with a look at the important process of molding character and preparing a teenager for life as a responsible, independent adult.

Fasten your seat belt, hold on tight, and enjoy the ride.

CHAPTER 1

◆◆◆ BODIES IN MOTION

You created my inmost being;
> you knit me together in my mother's womb.
I praise you because I am fearfully and wonderfully made;
> your works are wonderful,
> I know that full well.

PSALM 139:13-14

FROM A PHYSICAL STANDPOINT, the main event of adolescence is puberty, which serves as the physiological bridge between childhood and adulthood.

Puberty: the stage of maturation in which an individual becomes physiologically capable of sexual reproduction (from the Latin *puber*: "adult").

Rapid growth and body changes during these years are to a large degree brought about by interactions between several hormones: biochemical compounds created in one part of the body and sent via the bloodstream to have a specific effect somewhere else in the body. These chemical messages provoke an impressive number and variety of responses. Hormones and the glands that secrete them are collectively known as the *endocrine system*.

Not all hormones are related to reproduction. Thyroid hormone, for example, plays an important role in the body's metabolic rate. Insulin, which is secreted by the pancreas, escorts glucose (or blood sugar) into the cells that need and use this basic fuel. Growth hormone, as its name implies, is necessary for the attainment of normal adult height.

Speaking of growth hormone, a major growth spurt is one hallmark of adolescence, usually occurring between the ages of ten and fourteen in girls, and twelve and sixteen in boys. (Perhaps "spurt" isn't the most accurate term for this event, which actually lasts between two and three years.) The rate of growth can vary, but it tends to be fastest during spring and summer. Weight increases as well, and bones progress through their final stages of maturation. In addition, the percentage of body fat increases in girls and decreases in boys.

What physical changes can I expect in my son at puberty?

Male sexual development usually begins between the ages of ten and thirteen (the average age is eleven or twelve), and the process is usually completed in about three years, though it can range anywhere from two to five years. The timing and speed of bodily changes can vary greatly between boys of the same age, and boys who develop more slowly may need extra encouragement and continued reassurance that they will eventually reach the goal of manhood. A boy should be checked by his physician if he begins to show pubertal changes before age nine or has none of these developments underway by age fourteen.

The first physical sign of puberty in boys is enlargement of the testicles and thinning of the scrotum. Hair appears under the arms, on the face and chest, and in the genital area. His voice starts to deepen, although it may pass through an awkward phase of breaking, especially when he is excited or nervous.

The testicles begin manufacturing sperm, which are transported through a structure called the epididymis (one of which sits adjacent to each testicle) and then onward to the penis through a pair of flexible tubes called the vas deferens. The prostate begins to produce seminal fluid, which carries sperm out of the body during ejaculation.

The newly functioning sexual equipment will at times carry out its functions unexpectedly during the middle of the night in what is called a nocturnal emission or "wet dream," a normal event that an uninformed adolescent might find alarming. Along the same lines, boys may be concerned or embarrassed by unexpected erections, which can occur at very inopportune times (for example, just prior to giving a report in front of a class). Neither of these events should be interpreted as a sign of impending moral failure. In fact, it's best to brief your son about these normal occurrences before puberty arrives so he's not taken by surprise.

If you are a single mother who feels uncomfortable discussing these matters with your son, consider seeking help from an adult male who not only shares your values but has enough rapport to talk with your son about these topics.

Some boys develop a small, button-sized nodule of breast tissue directly under the nipple. This is a common response to changing hormones, although it may cause a minor panic when first discovered ("Is this a tumor?" "Am I going to develop breasts like a woman?"). This area may become a little tender but should return to normal within twelve to eighteen months. If you have any questions, or if breast tissue appears to be increasing in size (a phenomenon known as gynecomastia), have it checked by your son's doctor.

What physical changes can I expect in my daughter at this stage?

While pubertal development and the reproductive process are relatively straightforward in boys, the changes that take place as a girl progresses to womanhood are in many ways much more complex. (As you will see, they also take quite a bit longer to explain.) Not only does she undergo significant changes in her outward appearance, but inside her body a delicate interplay of hormones eventually leads to a momentous occasion: her first menstrual period (also called menarche), announcing her potential to reproduce.

The first visible sign of puberty in girls is the development of breast buds, which usually appear about two years before the first menstrual period. Each breast bud is a small, flat, firm button-like nodule that develops directly under the areola (the pigmented area that surrounds the nipple). This tissue eventually softens as the breasts enlarge. Occasionally a bud will develop on one side before the other, which might lead to the mistaken impression that a tumor is growing. But the passage of time and (if necessary) a doctor's examination will confirm that this growth is normal.

As the breasts continue to develop, hair begins to grow under the arms, on the legs, and in the genital area. The contour of the hips becomes fuller, and the internal reproductive organs grow and mature. Glands within the vagina produce a clear or milky secretion, which may appear several months before the onset of menstrual bleeding.

Finally, at the conclusion of an intricate sequence of hormonal events, the first menstrual flow arrives. This typically occurs around twelve or thirteen years of age, with a range between nine and sixteen. As with boys, girls who begin this process earlier or later than average will need some information and reassurance. In general, a girl should be checked by her physician if she develops breast buds before age eight or has her first period before age nine. At the opposite end of the spectrum, the absence of pubertal changes by thirteen or menstrual periods by sixteen should prompt a medical evaluation.

What goes on in my daughter's body during the menstrual cycle?

Under normal circumstances, each month a woman's body performs a three-act play titled *Preparing for a Baby*. What you are about to read is a summary of the essential characters and plot. (As with many other aspects of human physiology, there are thousands of other details that will not be spelled out here and thousands more yet to be discovered. The design of this process is indeed exquisite.)

The main characters in the play are:

- *The hypothalamus*: a multifaceted structure at the base of the brain that regulates basic bodily functions such as temperature and appetite. It also serves as the prime mover in the reproductive cycle.
- *The pituitary*: a small, punching-bag-shaped structure that appears to dangle from the brain directly below the hypothalamus. It has been called the "master gland" because it gives orders to many other organs. But it also takes important cues from the hypothalamus.
- *The ovaries*: a matched pair of organs in the female pelvis that serve two critical functions—releasing one or more eggs (or ova) each month and secreting the hormones estrogen and progesterone. At birth, the ovaries contain about two million eggs, a woman's lifetime supply. During childhood, the vast majority of these gradually disappear, and by the time a girl reaches puberty, only about 300,000 will be left. During a woman's reproductive years, she will release between three hundred and five hundred eggs; the rest will die and disappear.
- *The uterus*: a pear-shaped organ consisting primarily of muscle and containing a cavity where a baby grows during pregnancy. This cavity is lined with delicate tissue called

endometrium, which changes remarkably in response to the estrogen and progesterone produced by the ovaries. The uterus, also called the womb, is located at the top of the vagina and positioned in the middle of the pelvis between the bladder and the rectum.

- *The fallopian tubes*: a pair of tubes, about four to five inches (10 to 13 cm) long, attached to the upper corners of the uterus and extending toward each ovary. Their job is to serve as a meeting place for egg and sperm and then to transport a fertilized egg to the uterus.

Act I: Preparing an egg for launch (the follicular phase). The hypothalamus begins the monthly reproductive cycle by sending a "message" called *gonadotropin-releasing hormone* to the pituitary gland. The message says, in effect, "Send out the hormone that prepares an egg to be released by the ovaries." The pituitary responds by secreting into the bloodstream another biochemical message known as *follicle-stimulating hormone (FSH)*, which prepares an egg to be released by the ovaries. Each egg within an ovary is covered with a thin sheet of cells, and the term *follicle* (which literally means "little bag") refers to the entire package of egg and cells together. Under the influence of FSH, eight to ten follicles begin to grow and "ripen." Usually only one becomes dominant and progresses to full maturity.

This follicular phase of the cycle lasts about two weeks, during which the dominant follicle fills with fluid and enlarges to about three-quarters of an inch (2 cm). The egg contained within it will soon be released from the ovary. At the same time, this follicle secretes increasing amounts of estrogen, which (among other things) stimulates the lining of the uterus to proliferate and thicken. This is the first stage of preparation of the uterus for the arrival of a fertilized egg.

Act II: The egg is released (ovulation). As in Act I, this part of the story also begins in the hypothalamus. In response to rising levels of estrogen, the hypothalamus signals the pituitary to release a brief but intense surge of luteinizing hormone (LH) into the blood-stream. This hormone sets off a chain reaction in the ovaries. The dominant follicle enlarges, its outer wall becomes thin, and finally it ruptures, releasing egg and fluid. This mini-eruption, called ovulation, takes only a few minutes and occurs between twenty-four and forty hours after the peak of the LH surge. Sometimes a tiny amount of blood oozes from the ovary as well. This may irritate the lining of the abdomen, producing a discomfort known as *mittelschmerz* (German for "middle pain," because it occurs about halfway through the cycle).

Act III: The voyage of the egg and the preparation of the uterus (the luteal phase). The egg is not left to its own devices once it is set free from the ovary. At the end of each fallopian tube are struc-tures called *fimbriae* (Latin for "fingers"), whose delicate tentacles move over the area of the ovary. As soon as ovulation takes place, the fimbriae gently escort the egg into the tube, where it begins a journey toward the uterus. The cells that line the fallopian tube have microscopic hairlike projections called *cilia*, which move in a synchronized pattern and set up a one-way current through the tube. If sperm are present in the outer portion of the tube, and one of them is successful in penetrating the egg, fertilization takes place and a new life begins.

The fertilized egg will incubate in the tube for about three days before arriving at its destination, the cavity of the uterus, where it floats for approximately three more days before implant-ing. Around the seventh day, it "rests," implanting in the cavity of the uterus. If the egg is not fertilized, it will live only twelve to twenty-four hours and then disintegrate or pass through the tube and uterus into the vagina. (Since sperm live for forty-eight to seventy-two hours, there are three or four days in each cycle during which intercourse could lead to conception.)

Meanwhile, a lot of activity takes place in the ovary after ovulation. The newly vacated follicle has another job to do: prepare the uterus to accept and nourish a fertilized egg should one arrive. The follicle turns into a gland called the *corpus luteum* (literally, "yellow body," because cells lining the inside of the follicle develop a yellowish color), which secretes estrogen and, more important, progesterone, which dominates this luteal phase of the cycle, promoting growth and maturation of the uterine lining. This layer of tissue eventually doubles in thickness and becomes stocked with nutrients. Progesterone not only prepares the uterine "nursery" for a new arrival, but also relaxes the muscles of the uterus, decreasing the chance of contractions that might accidentally expel the egg. Progesterone also temporarily stops the preparation of any other eggs within the ovaries.

If a fertilized egg successfully implants and continues its growth within the uterus, it secretes a hormone called *human chorionic gonadotropin (HCG)*, which sends an important message to the corpus luteum: "Keep the hormones flowing!" The corpus luteum obliges and for nine or ten weeks continues to provide the hormonal support that allows the uterus to nourish the baby growing inside. After ten weeks, the placenta (the complex organ that connects the baby to the inner lining of the uterus) takes over the job of manufacturing progesterone, and the corpus luteum retires from active duty.

If there is no fertilization, no pregnancy, and thus no HCG, the corpus luteum degenerates. Progesterone and estrogen levels fall, resulting in a spasm of the blood vessels that supply the lining of the uterus. Deprived of the nutrients it needs to survive, the lining dies and passes from the uterus, along with blood and mucus, in what is called the menstrual flow (also referred to as a girl's "period" or menses).

Though the menstrual period might seem to be the end of the story, the first day of flow is actually counted as day one of a woman's reproductive cycle. For while the flow is taking place, the three-act play is starting over again as a new set of follicles begins to ripen in the ovaries. This "circle of life" will normally continue month after month throughout a girl's or woman's reproductive years, until menopause, unless it is interrupted by pregnancy or a medical condition that interferes with this cycle.

What is normal during menstrual periods?

The words *menstrual* and *menses* are derived from the Latin word for "month," which refers to the approximate frequency of this event. A typical cycle lasts from twenty-seven to thirty-five days, although for some women normal menses occurs as frequently as every twenty-one days or as infrequently as every forty-five days. Most of the variability arises during the first (follicular) phase leading up to ovulation. Assuming that a pregnancy does not begin, the luteal phase (from ovulation to menses) is nearly always fourteen days, with little variation.

For a year or two after a girl's first menstrual period, her cycles may be irregular because of anovulatory cycles, meaning an egg is not released. If ovulation does not take place, the cycle will remain stuck in the first (follicular) phase. Estrogen will continue to stimulate the lining of the uterus until some of it becomes so thick that it outgrows its blood supply. The shedding of this tissue resembles a menstrual period, but it is unpredictable and usually occurs with very little cramping. When ovulation finally takes place, the lining of the uterus will mature and then be shed all at once if a pregnancy has not started.

After a girl's first menstrual period, several months may pass before her endocrine system matures to the point of producing regular ovulation. During this time, it is not unusual for two or three months to pass between cycles. Because cramping doesn't normally occur unless ovulation has taken place, menstrual pains may not be noticed for months (or even one or two years) after the first cycle.

Menstrual flow typically lasts for three to six days, although very short (one-day) or longer (seven- or eight-day) periods may be normal for some women. One to three ounces (about 30 to 90 ml) of blood is usually lost during each cycle, though more or less than this amount may be a regular occurrence without any ill effects.

What should I tell my son if he asks about the menstrual cycle?

A boy should acquire some basic information about the female reproductive cycle in the course of learning how to treat the women in his life with care and respect. In order to protect boundaries of modesty (and prevent potential embarrassment), be careful about what is said and who is listening when discussing what is going on inside the body of your teenager. Generic comments ("When a woman is having her menstrual period . . .") are more appropriate than naming names ("When Jessica is having her menstrual period . . .").

What can be done to help menstrual cramps?

Menstrual cramps (the medical term is dysmenorrhea) most often are a by-product of the normal breakdown of the endometrium (lining of the uterus) at the end of a cycle. Chemicals, called prostaglandins, are released into the bloodstream by the endometrium, often with unpleasant effects. The most obvious response is a series of contractions of the muscles of the uterus, which may actually be as forceful as contractions during labor. During a strong contraction, blood may be inhibited from circulating throughout the uterine muscle, which, like any other muscle temporarily deprived of oxygen, will sound off with genuine pain. Prostaglandins may affect other parts of the body during a menstrual period, causing diarrhea, nausea, headaches, and difficulty with concentration. One bit of good news in connection with menstrual cramps is that they do *not* predict the level of pain a woman will feel during childbirth. In other words, a teenager with severe menstrual cramps will not necessarily have equally severe labor pains.

Menstrual cramps can be relieved in a variety of ways:

- Heating pads or warm baths are often helpful, for reasons that are unclear. (These may increase blood flow within the pelvis, improving the supply of oxygen to the uterine muscle.)
- Exercise and good general physical condition are often helpful in reducing cramps. Walking is a good exercise during this (or any) time of the month.
- Specific prostaglandin-inhibiting medications work well for many teens and older women alike. These are formulated to reduce the pain and inflammation of arthritis but have been found to also have a significant effect on menstrual cramps. Several are now available without prescription: ibuprofen (Advil, Motrin, Nuprin, and other brands), naproxen (Aleve), and ketoprofen (Orudis and others). These anti-inflammatory drugs should be taken with food to decrease the chance of stomach irritation. They are most effective if taken at the first sign of cramping and then continued on a regular basis (rather than "here and there" in response to pain) until the cramps stop. Your daughter's physician may recommend one of these medications (sometimes with a dosage schedule different from what is written on the package) or prescribe one of several other anti-inflammatory medications. Individual responses vary. If one type doesn't work well, another may seem like a miracle.

- Other pain-relief medications that may be helpful include the following:
  - ► Acetaminophen (Tylenol and others), which does not inhibit prostaglandins but can be quite effective nonetheless. Some women have found that alternating medications is helpful—for example, starting with ibuprofen, using acetaminophen for the next dose a few hours later, then switching back, and so on. *Note*: You should be aware that acetaminophen can be found in more than six hundred products (both prescription and over-the-counter), and that the total amount taken in any given day by an adult should not exceed 4000 mg. For children younger than twelve, or who weigh less than 110 pounds (50 kg), the maximum dose will be lower, based on weight. Check the label of any acetaminophen product for both the recommended dose and the amount of acetaminophen it contains—especially if this drug is present in more than one preparation you or other family members are using.
  - ► Midol has been marketed for decades as a treatment for discomforts associated with menstruation. Traditionally, it has included acetaminophen, caffeine, and the antihistamine pyrilamine, which not only may be mildly sedating, but may also have a modest diuretic effect (to reduce fluid retention). Today, Midol is a product line with several different formulations. Some of these substitute an anti-inflammatory drug (ibuprofen or naproxen) for acetaminophen. Some Midol products also contain pamabrom, another mild diuretic. If you plan to buy one of these products, *check the label* to be sure that its ingredients are not duplicating those found in other nonprescription remedies you may already be using.
  - ► If the discomfort of menstrual cramps cannot be

controlled by other measures, stronger pain relievers may be prescribed by a physician.

If menstrual cramps become disruptive and are unresponsive to home remedies and nonprescription medications, it is important that they be evaluated medically. Abnormalities of the cervix (the opening of the uterus) or the uterus itself, or a syndrome called *endometriosis* (in which tissue that normally lines the uterus grows in other parts of the body, usually in the pelvis) can on rare occasion be the cause of significant menstrual pain in an adolescent. If a medical examination finds no sign of endometriosis, the physician may prescribe diuretics and/or birth control pills (oral contraceptives).

Diuretics decrease fluid retention but do not directly relieve cramps; however, the discomfort may be less annoying if fluid retention is relieved.

Birth control pills may be helpful in reducing or eliminating significant cramps not adequately controlled by other means. In fact, for many teens, this may be the only type of medication helpful in reducing severe cramps that regularly interfere with normal activity. Each four-week cycle of pills provides three weeks of estrogen and progesterone in a specified amount. This prevents the LH surge and ovulation, and also usually results in less proliferation of the lining of the uterus than occurs during a normal cycle. During the fourth week, no hormones are present in the pills, allowing the lining to shed as in a normal cycle. However, the smaller amount of tissue involved usually generates less cramping. A variation on this approach, known as continuous oral contraception, extends the length of each cycle beyond twenty-eight days in order to reduce the number of menstrual periods.

A decision to use birth control pills should not be made casually. A medical evaluation to rule out other causes of pain may be necessary. (Indeed, if severe menstrual cramps continue while a woman is taking oral contraceptives, she should be reevaluated by her physician. Endometriosis is a definite possibility if this occurs.) Nausea, headaches, bloating, and/or worsening of acne are unpleasant side effects experienced by some users. (On the other hand, certain oral contraceptives can also improve acne.) The pills must be taken consistently each day to be effective.

The use of birth control pills may raise another concern, as well: Could taking them for menstrual cramps (or any other therapeutic purpose) indirectly lower your daughter's resistance to sexual activity? If you don't know the answer to this question, now is the time for candid conversation about sexuality. For a girl who is fervently committed to remaining abstinent, it would be unfortunate to withhold a treatment that might reduce debilitating pain just because of a parent's vague mistrust. Furthermore, the decision to postpone sex until marriage should be built on a strong, multilayered foundation. If the absence of contraceptives is the only reason your daughter is avoiding intercourse, she needs to hear and understand many more reasons.

Should I be concerned if my daughter has irregular periods?

Irregular menstrual periods may be a cause for concern if they are

- too rare, occurring every three or four months after more than a year has passed since the first period.
- too frequent, with bleeding or spotting occurring throughout the month.
- too long, lasting more than seven or eight consecutive days.
- too heavy, soaking through more than six to eight pads or tampons per day.

For any of these problems, a medical evaluation is usually indicated to discover the underlying cause. In many instances, the diagnosis will be anovulatory cycles resulting from an immature endocrine system. But other physical or even emotional events can also interfere with the complex interaction of hormones that brings about the monthly cycle. These include:

- *Medical disorders.* These could include malfunctions of the endocrine system (including pituitary, adrenal, or thyroid glands) or abnormalities of the ovaries, uterus, or vagina.
- *Significant changes in weight.* Obese teens can generate enough estrogen in their fat cells to affect the lining of the uterus. At the opposite extreme, stringent diets or the severe reduction of food intake seen with anorexia nervosa will effectively shut down the menstrual cycle (see the questions on eating disorders, beginning on page 158).
- *Extreme levels of exercise.* Female athletes with demanding training programs may have infrequent periods, or their cycles may stop altogether.
- *Stress.* Stormy emotional weather is not uncommon during the adolescent years, and personal upheavals can cause a teenage girl to miss one or more periods.
- *Pregnancy.* In some cases, an unexpected absence of menstrual cycles indicates that pregnancy has begun.

It is important that extremes in menstrual flow (whether too much or too little) be evaluated. Not only may the underlying cause have great significance, but the menstrual irregularity could also have damaging consequences of its own. For example, very frequent or heavy bleeding may outstrip an adolescent's ability to replenish red blood cells. Iron deficiency can develop when there is an inadequate amount of iron in the diet to keep up with what is being lost in menstrual blood flow each month. This not only can cause ongoing fatigue and poor concentration in school, but may also lead to anemia—a shortage of red blood cells (which are also smaller and contain less hemoglobin, the oxygen-carrying molecule) that can result in light-headedness or even fainting episodes.

Absence of menstrual periods related to a continual failure to ovulate may result in months or years of nonstop estrogen stimulation of the uterus. Without the maturing effect of progesterone, the lining of the uterus may be at increased risk for developing precancerous abnormalities. This scenario is one of the concerns for women (of all ages) with *polycystic ovary syndrome*, a metabolic disturbance usually characterized by infrequent menstrual periods as well as excessive weight and body hair.

Teens whose cycles stop because of weight loss or intense physical training (or both) may suffer an irreversible loss of bone density, known as *osteoporosis*. Normally a problem faced by women much later in life (typically well after menopause), osteoporosis can lead to disabling fractures of the spine, hips, wrists, and other bones.

It is impossible to state a single course of action that will resolve all the various forms of menstrual irregularity. However, if there appears to be no underlying disturbance that needs specific treatment and the problem is determined to be irregular ovulation, a doctor may recommend hormonal treatment to regulate the cycle. This may take the form of progesterone, which can be given at a defined time each month to bring on a menstrual period. As an alternative, birth control pills may be recommended to restore order by overriding a woman's own cycle and establishing one that is more predictable. As mentioned earlier, the decision to use this type of medication in an adolescent must be made with particular care and discernment.

What are PMS and PMDD?

Prior to menstruation, most women experience some degree of discomfort, which may occur for a day or two or may extend over the entire two-week period following ovulation. Mild physical or emotional distress during this time, sometimes called *premenstrual tension*, is very common. But 20 to 40 percent of women experience symptoms severe enough to disrupt normal activities. This is commonly called *premenstrual syndrome*, or *PMS*.

A specific cause for PMS has not been identified, but the effects are all too familiar for many women, including teens. Physical symptoms can include bloating and fullness in the abdomen, fluid retention (with tightness of rings and shoes), headaches, breast tenderness, backache, fatigue, and dizziness. More dramatic are the emotional symptoms: irritability, anxiety, depression, poor concentration, insomnia, difficulty making decisions, and unusual food cravings. These can occur in various combinations and levels of severity. The most striking feature is usually the instability and intensity of negative emotions, which can send other family members running for cover. Some teenagers and older women feel like Dr. Jekyll and Ms. Hyde—calm and rational for the first two weeks of the cycle and out of control for the second two weeks, with dramatic improvement once the menstrual flow commences. Between 3 and 5 percent of women have premenstrual emotional storms severe enough to cause significant disturbances at home, school, or work, a condition designated in recent years as *premenstrual dysphoric disorder*, or *PMDD*.

What treatments are useful for PMS or PMDD?

A few decades ago, PMS was considered primarily a psychological event, an "adjustment reaction" to reproductive issues or life in general. This is no longer the case. PMS should be taken as seriously as any other physical issue. Though no quick-fix remedies or lifetime cures exist for PMS, a number of measures can help your adolescent (and others at home) reduce its impact:

Make sure the emotional and physical symptoms are, in fact, PMS. Adolescent emotions are often intense and variable, and other life issues (involving school, friends, family, etc.) may be at the heart of the problem. If there is any question, symptoms can be charted on a calendar, along with menstrual periods, for two or three months. You should see an improvement for at least a week following menses. Symptoms that continue well after a period is over or throughout the cycle involve something other than (or in addition to) PMS, including possible depression. Keep in mind that PMS, or PMDD, can be superimposed on an ongoing depression, and turbulent emotions can take a marked turn for the worse— even including suicidal thoughts—during the week or two prior to menses. Anyone whose thinking turns to self-harm, even if it occurs only during certain times of the month, should be evaluated and treated immediately. (For more information about this important topic, see the questions on depression, starting on page 166.)

Keep the lines of communication open and plan ahead. Once your daughter's cycle is well established, she will be able to predict when the more troublesome days are coming. This may give others at home advance "storm warning," enabling them to respond to her with an extra measure of TLC, or at least to cut her a little slack. This is particularly important if more than one person at home has difficulty with PMS, because the collision of two unstable moods can be quite unpleasant. If your daughter is currently irritable because of the time of the month, and a change for the better is likely in the immediate future, you would be wise to postpone any conversations about emotionally charged issues for a few days if possible. At the same time, while it is important to acknowledge the reality of PMS symptoms, they shouldn't be allowed to become a blanket excuse for blatant disrespect, acting out, or abandonment of responsibilities.

Encourage sensible eating and exercise. Frequent, smaller meals may help prevent bloating, and avoiding salt can reduce fluid retention. Caffeine may increase irritability, so decaffeinated drinks (and medications) are more appropriate. All-around physical conditioning through the entire month can improve general well-being and play a major role in helping a woman navigate more smoothly to the end of a cycle.

In addition, a variety of remedies, nutritional supplements, and medications have been recommended at one time or another for this problem. Some have a more consistent track record (and better scientific support) than others, and your adolescent should consider getting advice from her physician before trying any of these. Keep in mind that megadoses of any vitamin or mineral— quantities that greatly exceed the recommended dietary allowance (RDA)—are not advised for this condition. The bottom line for any PMS treatment is an honest assessment of the effectiveness, safety, and side effects for the individual taking it.

- *Nonprescription medications* such as acetaminophen or ibuprofen to reduce aches and pains may be of some help.
- *Calcium* (1200 mg per day) and *magnesium* (200 mg per day) supplements have both been shown to reduce symptoms of PMS (especially physical discomforts) by 40 to 50 percent. Improvements may not be noticed, however, until two or three cycles have passed while taking the supplements.
- *Vitamin E* supplements (usually at 400 IU per day, but no more than that) have shown mixed results in research studies on PMS.
- *Vitamin B_6*, which has long been advocated as a remedy for PMS symptoms, has performed poorly in controlled studies and probably has limited usefulness at best. If numbness or tingling of the hands or feet occur while taking this vitamin, it should be discontinued.
- A number of *herbal preparations* have been advocated for

one or more symptoms of PMS, but research studies investigating such claims have yielded mixed results. Evening primrose oil and ginkgo biloba, for example, have not been shown to be effective. Dry extracts of agnus castus fruit (also called chasteberry) improved symptoms in one study.[1] If you are considering an herbal remedy for your adolescent, keep in mind that the Food and Drug Administration (FDA) does not certify herbal preparations for safety or effectiveness.

- *Prescription medications* most widely used for PMS fall into three basic categories: diuretics, antidepressants, and hormonal manipulators. Obviously, the use of any of these will require evaluation and follow-up by a physician.

  ▸ *Diuretics.* For many women, much of the discomfort from PMS arises from bloating and fluid retention, so the use of a mild diuretic (or "water pill") to maintain normal fluid levels during the second half of each cycle can be effective.

  ▸ *Antidepressants.* Many PMS symptoms, and certainly those of PMDD, duplicate those seen in depression. Some women with severe PMS fight milder forms of the same emotional symptoms throughout the month. It now appears that the fundamental physiological problem in PMS involves changes in the levels of biological messengers in the brain known as *neurotransmitters*.

    New research has shown significant reduction in PMS symptoms with a specific family of antidepressants called *selective serotonin reuptake inhibitors (SSRIs),* such as fluoxetine (Prozac or Sarafem), sertraline (Zoloft), paroxetine (Paxil), citalopram (Celexa), and others. Often, doses lower than those needed to treat depression are effective in reducing PMS/PMDD symptoms, and many women obtain satisfactory results by taking one of these medications on an intermittent basis, typically seven to ten days each month. Though these drugs are safe and well tolerated for the vast majority who use them, and definitely *not* habit-forming, individual responses and side effects can vary considerably—especially in teens.

Before your daughter starts a prescription (or takes samples from her doctor), it is essential to have a careful discussion with her health-care provider about the potential benefits and problems associated with SSRIs. It is particularly important to report any *increase* in irritability or agitation in a teenager who is taking this type of medication. (For more information, see chapter 6.)

▸ *Hormonal manipulation* has been utilized with variable success, though this is not commonly prescribed for teens with PMS. Women who take supplemental progesterone during the second half of the menstrual cycle may report marked improvement, a worsening of symptoms (especially depression), or no effect at all. Though supplemental progesterone is heavily promoted on the Internet and radio infomercials as a treatment for PMS, most research studies have shown it to be no more effective than a placebo.[2] (A substance that provides no greater relief than a placebo is generally considered ineffective.) Hormonal preparations should be utilized in teens only after thoughtful consideration of the pros and cons by patient, parent, and physician.

Which is best for my daughter: pad or tampon?

From the very first to the final reproductive cycle, either tampons or external pads may be used to absorb menstrual flow. Each has its specific advantages and disadvantages. Deodorant pads and tampons and feminine hygiene sprays may irritate delicate tissue, and douching is unnecessary and should be avoided. Any persistent drainage that is discolored, itchy, painful, or foul-smelling should be evaluated by a physician.

External pads may be more comfortable for a young adolescent who feels uneasy about inserting a foreign object into her vagina. However, pads may cause heat and moisture to be retained around the external genital area (especially in hot or humid climates) and increase the likelihood of local irritation or infection.

Tampons allow more freedom of activity (especially for vigorous exercise or swimming) and less chance of contributing to external irritation. Some parents may worry about tampons causing damage inside or at the opening of the vagina; however, inserting a tampon does not tear the hymen (the ring of soft tissue just inside the labia at the entrance to the vagina), although difficulty inserting tampons may be the first indication of an abnormality of this structure. Very rarely, small vaginal ulcerations may result from improper tampon insertion.

Of more concern is the association of tampon use with toxic shock syndrome (TSS), a condition caused by a toxin produced by *Staphylococcus aureus* bacteria. A number of cases occurred in the 1980s in connection with a particular type of tampon that appeared to foster the growth of *S. aureus* in the vagina and irritate the vaginal lining. This tampon was taken off the market, but subsequent evidence has indicated that the primary risk factors for the development of TSS are the amount of time a tampon is left in place near the opening of the vagina, and the size and absorbency of the tampon.

Most symptoms of this problem are nonspecific: fever, chills, headache, muscle aches, vomiting, diarrhea, and faintness (caused by a drop in blood pressure). A more specific sign is a sunburn-like rash on the palms and soles. When severe, toxic shock syndrome is treated in the hospital with large doses of antibiotics as well as fluids given intravenously to maintain blood pressure. The development of flu-like symptoms and light-headedness—feeling faint or actually passing out, especially associated with standing up or other changes in position—may be very significant if they occur during a menstrual period. These symptoms should be evaluated by a physician *as soon as possible.*

Fortunately, TSS is rare. (Some *S. aureus* or *Streptococcus* bacterial infections may provoke TSS in situations that do not involve tampon use, and thus may occur in either males or females.) Most physicians believe that tampons are safe for both teens and older women, although fifteen- to nineteen-year-olds have the highest risk for developing toxic shock syndrome from tampon use. Simple precautions can markedly reduce this risk.

First, and most important, don't leave a tampon in place for more than six hours. Follow the manufacturer's instructions closely. Insert (and remove) tampons carefully. Store tampons in a clean, dry place. Wash hands before inserting or removing tampons. Use tampons with the least absorbency necessary to control the flow. Tampons are now graded for absorbency as follows: light, regular, super, super plus, and ultra. (Super plus and ultra are not recommended for use by teens.)

Less absorbent tampons are smaller and less likely to irritate the lining of the vagina. If a tampon is difficult to remove, shreds, doesn't need to be changed for several hours, or is associated with vaginal dryness, a smaller size should be used.

Consider alternating tampons and pads during the same menstrual period. (For example, use tampons during the day—changing them every few hours—and pads at night.)

What tests are usually done in a routine physical exam?

During the next few years, your teenager will probably need medical input on a number of occasions, including screening exams for sports, camp, and general health assessment. Injuries arising from sports or other vigorous activities may need attention. Problems related to menstruation may require medical evaluation and intervention. In addition, a variety of symptoms and emotional concerns may arise during these years.

Adolescent health-care guidelines recommend yearly visits to the doctor for assessment, screening, and guidance, even if there have been other evaluations during the year for specific medical problems. Quick exams for camp or sports, especially those done assembly-line style on large groups of teens, are no substitute for a more comprehensive physical exam by your regular health-care provider. If there are special health problems, more frequent exams may be necessary.

Most doctors will talk with parent and teen together during the visit, but part of the time will be spent without the parent present. This is usually done to increase the likelihood that the doctor is receiving accurate information, with the assumption that many teenagers may feel uncomfortable answering sensitive questions in front of their parents. It is customary during this time alone for a physician to assure the young patient of the confidentiality of their conversation. (When abuse is suspected, however, the health-care provider must notify the appropriate local social-service agency. Also, if there appears to be an imminent threat of suicide, referral to a qualified counselor, psychiatrist, or mental-health facility will be necessary.) *It is therefore extremely important that you consider carefully who is going to provide health care for your adolescent.*

Ideally, your teenager's health-care provider will not only be medically competent, but also someone whom your teenager trusts and can talk with comfortably; whom *you* trust; who knows you and your family; and who shares your basic values.

The last qualification is particularly significant because of the near certainty that your teenager will eventually be in a one-on-one situation with the physician. Your son or daughter may feel more comfortable discussing sensitive topics with a doctor than with you, even if you have an extremely close and honest relationship. You will want to be certain that the advice and counsel given behind closed doors, especially regarding sexual behavior, will not contradict or undermine principles you have been teaching at home. During these critical years, everyone needs to be on the same team.

Although teens usually have an interest in discussing a variety of topics with their doctors, they may feel embarrassed to broach certain subjects. The physician should have the interest (and time) to ask some probing questions and then offer sound input based on the response. (There is no guarantee, of course, that a teenager will tell "the whole truth and nothing but," even when confidentiality is assured.) Along with questions about past history and any current symptoms, specific topics that are usually on the physician's agenda (if not on the patient's) include the following:

- Growth and development. Younger teens are particularly concerned about whether they are normal, especially if pubertal changes are taking place earlier or later than in their peers.
- Physical safety, including the use of seat belts, bicycle or motorcycle helmets, and appropriate sports equipment.
- Current dietary practices. Are they healthy, erratic, or extreme in any way?
- Immunization history and updates.
- Exercise and sleep. Is there enough of each?
- Tobacco use.
- Alcohol and drug use.
- Sexual activity.
- Relationships at home and school.
- The emotional climate. Are there any signs of depression?
- Sexual or other physical abuse. A physician who is attentive to an adolescent's physical well-being and demeanor may be the first to detect signs of abuse. By law, physicians are required to report any concerns about abuse to the appropriate local social-service or law-enforcement agency.

In addition to the usual elements of a medical exam (ears, throat, neck, chest, heart, abdomen), a few other areas are also important:

- Blood pressure. Though hypertension (elevated blood pressure) is not common in teens, if detected it must be evaluated further.
- The spine. Special attention is given to scoliosis, a sideways curvature of the spine. There are specific guidelines regarding the degree of curvature that help determine whether treatment is needed, and if so, what methods might be appropriate.
- The groin area should be checked for hernias (primarily in boys).
- The testes should be checked for appropriate development and for any abnormal masses. Testicular cancer is unique for its prevalence among young men, and teenagers should get in the habit of a brief monthly self-check for unusual growths in this area.
- The breasts in both sexes.

Some additional tests may be done during a basic physical exam. These could include the following:

- Vision and hearing screening
- Urinalysis
- Blood tests, such as a blood count to check for anemia (especially in girls), or screening for cholesterol and other circulating fat molecules (called lipids) if there is a history of elevated cholesterol or heart attack before age fifty-five in one or more family members
- A screening test for tuberculosis (TB) may be put on the

arm if there is a risk of prior exposure to this infection, or if required for school or college entrance.

What about immunizations?

A number of immunization updates are usually given during the adolescent years.

A vaccine called Tdap, which provides booster immunization against *tetanus, diphtheria*, and *whooping cough* (pertussis), may be given as early as age ten, but no later than ten years after the previous tetanus booster (which was probably given at age four or five as DTaP, the combination given to infants and children up to six years of age). Thereafter, tetanus immunizations are normally repeated every ten years throughout one's life. A booster may be given after five years if one sustains a wound from a puncture, crush injury, burn, or frostbite, or a wound contaminated with dirt, feces, or saliva. Some physicians recommend a tetanus booster if five years have elapsed since the previous one and the adolescent is going on a wilderness expedition or to a foreign country where the vaccine might not be available.

Meningococcus vaccine should be given if it was not included during an earlier immunization visit (at age eleven or twelve).

Measles/mumps/rubella (MMR) vaccine should be given if your adolescent had only one such injection during infancy or child-hood. (Normally one dose is given between one year and fifteen months, and a second between four and six years of age.) If your teenager has never received this vaccine, two doses should be given, separated by a minimum of four weeks.

Hepatitis A and/or *hepatitis B* vaccines should be given if one (or both) series has not already been completed. Most teens have received a hepatitis B series during infancy or prior to admission to kindergarten. Routine vaccination against hepatitis A is a more recent recommendation, but it is particularly important for teens to complete a series of two doses if they are planning to travel extensively, especially to rural or impoverished areas of foreign countries.

If your adolescent has never had *chicken pox* (*varicella*) and has not been immunized against it, vaccination against this virus is advisable, especially because infections in teenagers and adults tend to be more severe than in younger children. Two doses of varicella vaccine are recommended, separated by at least four weeks for a teenager (thirteen years and older) or by at least three months for a child seven to twelve years of age. If your child previously had one dose of vaccine, now is the time for a booster. Varicella vaccine may be given at the same time as an MMR and/or Tdap injection. However, if varicella and MMR are not given simultaneously, an interval of at least a month should separate the two.

The *influenza* virus makes an annual appearance in most communities during the winter, provoking fever, aches, and coughing that are often more intense than a garden-variety upper-respiratory infection. Though most teens recover from influenza after a few days of rest, fluids, and acetaminophen for their aches and pains, this illness can derail a teen's activities for several days. Furthermore, those with significant medical problems such as heart disease, diabetes, or chronic respiratory disturbances (especially asthma) may suffer severe complications. The CDC now recommends that everyone over six months of age (including healthy teenagers) receive a flu vaccine every year. Because new strains of this virus appear annually, a new vaccine must be prepared each year and is typically given during the fall.

You should check with your doctor if you have any questions about the advisability of these immunizations. This is particularly important if your adolescent has a significant medical issue, especially one that affects the function of the immune system (for example, leukemia, symptomatic HIV disease, pregnancy, or a cancer under treatment with chemotherapy). Be sure to inquire about precautions or potential side effects of any vaccine your teenager might be given.

What about the human papillomavirus (HPV) vaccine?

HPV is the most common sexually transmitted infection in the United States, with approximately twenty million Americans infected.[3] There are approximately one hundred types of HPV, of which about thirty are sexually transmitted.[4] Most people who are infected with the virus have no symptoms and the infection clears up without intervention. Other people, however, can develop genital warts and precancerous changes in cells in the cervix, vulva, anus, or penis. Still other infections progress to cancer in these and other areas. HPV is the primary cause of more than 99 percent of cervical cancers,[5] and is implicated as a cause of 30 to 50 percent of cancers of the mouth and throat.[6] The American Cancer Society estimated that in 2011 more than 12,000 women would be diagnosed with cervical cancer and nearly 4,300 women would die from the disease.[7] In addition, it was projected that about 34,000 new cases of mouth and throat cancer would be diagnosed in 2011, and nearly 7,000 would die from this disease. (This form of cancer occurs about twice as often in men as in women.)[8]

Two vaccines now available can prevent infection with the subtypes of HPV most commonly associated with cervical cancer. Cervarix targets two types of the virus and has been approved only for females. Gardasil provides immunity for four types of HPV and has been approved for use in both males and females. Gardasil also protects females against most genital warts, as well as anal, vaginal, and vulvar cancers. Furthermore, it protects males against genital warts and most anal cancers. HPV vaccination is now recommended for girls and boys at age eleven or twelve, though it may be given as early as age nine and as late as age twenty-six. It is given in a three-dose series, with the second dose given one to two months after the first, and the third dose six months after the first.

While the thought of giving your school-age child a vaccine to protect against a sexually transmitted virus might be unsettling, there are a number of good reasons to consider doing so:

- The immune response is more robust when the vaccine is given at a younger age.
- Girls and boys in this age group are not likely to have been exposed to HPV infection.
- Even if an adolescent makes and keeps a commitment to sexual abstinence until marriage, there is no guarantee that the person he or she marries will have done so, nor is it possible to determine whether the other person is carrying (and could transmit) one of the high-risk HPV viruses. Furthermore, if your child were to become the victim of a sexual assault, the attacker could be carrying one or more of the high-risk viruses.
- The HPV immunization process presents an opportunity for parents and children to have candid, ongoing conversations about sexuality before the onset of adolescence. A girl or boy receiving the vaccine should understand that it does not protect against all strains of HPV, nor against other sexually transmitted organisms, and that reserving sexual activity for marriage is the healthiest decision she or he can make—physically, emotionally, and spiritually. For further guidance regarding teenage sexuality, see chapter 4.

When should a girl receive her first pelvic exam?

Most medical authorities recommend a pelvic exam for a girl or young woman

- within three years of the onset of sexual activity;
- if she has symptoms or concerns about disease—such as

vaginal discharge, pelvic pain, or other pelvic symptoms, which normally cannot be diagnosed by history alone;
- if she is going to be married in the near future;
- if she is going to start on birth control pills for any reason;
- by the age of twenty-one, even if she is not sexually active or has no specific concerns.

No adolescent girl (or any older woman, for that matter) is excited about having a pelvic exam, especially if there is already discomfort in this area. It is important that the practitioner explain the process step-by-step and then talk the patient through the procedure while it is being done. Reassure your daughter that it is normal to feel nervous and awkward, and make sure she knows that though the exam is not particularly comfortable, it should not be extremely painful either. Both you and your daughter should understand that a pelvic exam does not compromise her virginity. Sexual morality is not violated by a medical procedure whose purpose is to assess, diagnose, and treat potential physical problems.

Your daughter should feel free to tell her physician when and where it hurts and know that the exam will be modified if she is having a lot of pain. Many teenagers feel more comfortable if the exam is done by a physician they know and trust, regardless of gender, while others prefer that it be done by a female health-care provider. In either case, the examiner should be accompanied by a female attendant.

Normally during a pelvic exam, the external genitals are briefly inspected, and then a speculum (the "duckbill" instrument) is gently inserted. A narrow speculum should be available for younger patients, and this should pass through the hymen (the ring of soft tissue just inside the labia at the entrance to the vagina) without tearing it. The vaginal walls will be checked, and a Pap test (smear) is normally done.

This painless test collects cells from the cervix (the opening of the uterus) to check for abnormalities that might indicate an increased risk for developing cancer in this area (or, in rare cases among teenagers, the actual presence of cancer). Using a wooden or plastic spatula, the outer surface of the cervix is scraped, and a swab or thin brush is used to collect cells for testing. These specimens may be spread on microscope slides or placed in a liquid preparation before being placed on a slide. The latter approach, called a "thin prep" Pap, is more likely to remove extraneous debris from the specimen and spread the cells more evenly.

However it is prepared, the slide will be read by a specially trained technologist or pathologist—a physician who, among other things, is an expert at identifying abnormalities in cells.

Test results typically fall into one of three categories: normal, abnormal but not yet cancerous, or highly likely to be cancerous. Thin-prep Pap tests can also identify specific types of the human papillomavirus (HPV) associated with cancer of the cervix, and even diagnose two other sexually transmitted infections: gonorrhea and chlamydia. Action taken in response to an abnormal Pap test will depend on several factors, including the severity of the changes observed.

After taking the Pap test specimen, the examiner will insert one or two fingers into the vagina while the other hand gently presses on the lower abdomen. Much information can be obtained from this simple maneuver, including the size of the uterus and ovaries and the location and intensity of any tenderness. A rectal examination may also be done at this time.

What should I do if my teenager has recurring vague physical symptoms?

You may at times become frustrated by ongoing vague physical complaints ("I don't feel well . . ."), especially those that sound very compelling in the morning yet seem to evaporate by midafternoon. How do you know whether to offer TLC and bed rest or send your teenager off to school? The answer isn't always easy. More than once you may struggle with guilt after discovering your child really *was* sick but you had overruled his protests and made him attend classes. On other occasions, you may be compassionate in the morning and then feel as if you've been taken advantage of when your teenager makes a "miraculous recovery" at the end of the school day.

If symptoms are frequent, ask your health-care provider to help sort things out. To get the most out of this consultation, spend time before the visit talking over the problem with your teenager, listing the problems (fatigue, headaches) and their characteristics (how often, how long, what helps, what makes it worse).

While you're at it, try to get a feel for the social climate at school, in the neighborhood, or at church. Questions with no obvious right or wrong answer ("Who do you like to hang around with?" or "What's your least favorite class?") may open the window to some current events and possibly tip you off about pressures that might be contributing to the symptoms.

Ultimately, your teen's doctor will need to ask some specific questions, perhaps including a little gentle probing into the issues of the patient's daily life. If the medical evaluation uncovers a specific diagnosis, be sure that both you and your adolescent understand what should be done about it—including the parameters for going to school versus staying home. If the problem doesn't appear to be an ongoing physical illness, develop a game plan for dealing with mornings when your teenager doesn't feel well and agree on the ground rules for school attendance.

If you uncover personal issues that are contributing to physical symptoms, don't shy away from working toward solutions. Whether it's a hard-nosed teacher, a hallway bully, an acute absence of friendships, or some other emotion-jarring problem, your teenager needs to feel your support and know you will help to find an answer. Making progress in one or more of these areas will typically go a long way toward shortening the list of symptoms.

CHAPTER 2

STRIVING FOR INDEPENDENCE

A wise son brings joy to his father,
   but a foolish son grief to his mother.
PROVERBS 10:1

FOR CENTURIES, TEENAGERS have routinely challenged and at times exasperated their parents. Public and private turmoil about what to do about the younger generation is not unique to our moment in history, nor are most of the fundamental concerns that adolescents will encounter during their eventful passage into adulthood. This chapter will deal with many aspects of that important process, along with a number of parenting attitudes and strategies that can help teenagers navigate adolescence in a positive and productive way.

When your child was a newborn, her short nights of sleep, dirty diapers, and crying spells may have hampered your ability to marvel at the incredible little person before you. When she was a turbocharged and at times defiant toddler, the nonstop effort required to keep her (and your home) safe and sound may not have given you much time to appreciate her rapidly developing abilities. Similarly, when your adolescent experiences normal growing pains and emotional turbulence (and possibly a crisis or two) during the coming years, it may be all too easy to lose sight of a number of very encouraging and gratifying developments.

Yes, there will be a lot of problems to solve, arriving in all shapes and sizes (often when you least expect them). You will need to guide, monitor, and sometimes intervene to keep the cultural wolves a respectable distance from your teenager's door. You may have to put out some fires or even an occasional four-alarm blaze. Hopefully, through it all you will be able to recognize and appreciate in your adolescent many of the positive attributes that are common in this age group:

- energy and enthusiasm
- idealism
- concern for the needs of others—often coupled with a willingness to offer help in ways that adults might find risky or "unrealistic"
- desire for meaningful relationships
- a sense of humor that can be witty and insightful
- concern for fairness and justice
- interest in other cultures and countries
- development of new skills in athletics, the arts, crafts, the use of tools, writing, and speaking—often with extraordinary achievements
- curiosity—not only about the way things work in the world, but also *why*
- willingness to commit to worthwhile causes and to back up that commitment with specific actions
- ability (and attention span) to appreciate sophisticated music, drama, films, and artwork
- a deep desire for a relationship with God and a willingness to make a lifelong commitment to serve Him

How and when these qualities will be expressed will vary with each individual, but be on the lookout for them—and be sure to express your appreciation when they appear.

Despite the relatively few years separating one generation from the next, most adults seem to have amnesia about their own adolescence. Parents who have already "been there, done that" may have difficulty recalling how they felt and thought between the ages of twelve and twenty-one. As you read through the stages of adolescent development in the next few pages, try to recall what you experienced during those years. Whether your effort brings fond memories, a lot of pain, or merely a sigh of relief that you don't have to go through those experiences again, you will connect more smoothly with your son or daughter if you can remember what it's like to be a teenager.

With rare exception, adolescents develop a powerful drive to become independent, to be in charge of their daily affairs and their future. As a result, bucking the limits, challenging authority, and resisting constraints imposed at home and at school are pretty much par for the course. And though your teen's behavior may seem outrageous, some degree of struggling against parental control is a normal and necessary part of growing up.

Your job in helping your adolescent complete this task is to release your grip in a controlled and reasonable manner. You still have the right and responsibility to make house rules. But when you impose (and defend) them, you need to do so calmly and respectfully. "Because I'm the Mom, that's why!" may have worked with your two-year-old, but it will rarely be appropriate now. Few things exasperate and discourage a teenager more than being treated like an immature child, even if it may seem appropriate (to you) at the time.

Even more important is linking your adolescent's blossoming independence to the realities and responsibilities of adult life. He will need hundreds of age-appropriate reality checks before he leaves your nest, and you are in the best position to provide them.

What are the three stages of adolescence?

There are many important differences between a twelve-year-old seventh grader and a nineteen-year-old college student, and so it is helpful to divide the adolescent years into three developmental phases:

- Early adolescence—ages twelve through fourteen (junior high/middle school)
- Middle adolescence—ages fifteen through seventeen (senior high)
- Late adolescence—ages eighteen through twenty-one (college/vocation)

Each adolescent's life will run on a unique track, of course, and all sorts of variations on the basic themes will occur during each phase. Some junior high students may appear intellectually and emotionally ready for college, while some college students behave as if junior high were still in session. Some thirteen-year-olds are immune to the opinions of their peers, and some twenty-one-year-olds' convictions change with each day's companions. But familiar trends and behaviors about each of the three phases are generally recognizable.

What changes are likely to occur during early adolescence (the middle school years)?

All too frequently, a relatively well-adjusted, good-natured child enters the sixth or seventh grade and two or three years later emerges emotionally (if not physically) battered and bruised. What turns these years into such a war zone?

The tides of puberty are likely to be flowing at full speed. Among other things, these generate much concern and self-consciousness about physical changes that are (or aren't yet) under way. Such worries are intensified by the marked variations in development at this age.

Wide mood swings and strong emotional responses to the ups and downs of life are the order of the day. Physical and hormonal components contribute to this stormy weather in both sexes, although the biochemistry of the monthly cycle can accentuate the mood swings in girls.

Emotional reactions to life's twists and turns, even in a stable home environment, can provoke physical responses as well, especially headaches, abdominal pains, and fatigue. Though any of these may be caused by the daily strain of growing up, they should be evaluated by a physician if persistent or disruptive.

In addition to these physical and emotional upheavals among individual adolescents, bringing many of them together (as occurs every school day) creates a social stew containing large doses of volatile ingredients:

- An intense need for acceptance by peers
- An equally intense concern about looking dumb, clumsy, or at all different from the surrounding herd of other early adolescents—who themselves are intensely concerned about looking dumb, clumsy, or at all different from everyone else
- An ongoing struggle with self-confidence or overt feelings of inferiority, even among those who are the most attractive and talented (or tough and hostile)
- A surprising—and at times shocking—intolerance for anyone who looks or behaves a little unlike everyone else
- A limitless capacity for creative (and often obscene) insults, put-downs, and jokes directed at nearly everyone—but

especially the one who is different. This is particularly and sometimes painfully obvious in group settings.

Consequently, school represents more than classroom activities and homework for many adolescents. It can be a daily social gauntlet—unpleasant at best, a barbaric ordeal at worst—requiring every ounce of effort and energy just to complete the round-trip back to home base.

While you might expect your young adolescent to come to you for aid and comfort or to take cover from the daily shellings at school, the opposite may take place. The budding (or broiling) urge for independence, combined with mood swings, extreme self-consciousness, and intolerance for anything deemed "stupid" or "lame," may begin to drive an alarming wedge into your relationship.

Early adolescents typically form and maintain strong same-sex friendships, even as interest in members of the opposite sex is growing more intense. Infatuations and crushes are to be expected, but intense romances and dating are not good at this age for a number of reasons.

As already mentioned, friends and peers can play a major role in reinforcing or undermining the values that matter to you. You may become frustrated that a classmate's half-baked opinions seem to matter more than all the common sense you've imparted over the years. But choose wisely if you decide to intervene, because the more you complain about your teenager's newfound friends, the more vigorously she may defend them.

While the value of your parental stock may seem to fall by the hour, you may be surprised (and perhaps a little hurt) to see your adolescent form a powerful attachment to another adult, such as a teacher, choir director, favorite aunt, coach, or youth leader. This can be a blessing if the object of this affection is an ally who shares your values and goals and who moves your teenager in positive directions. But someone with a less constructive agenda can have a significant negative impact.

What changes are likely to occur during middle adolescence (the high school years)?

For many adolescents and their parents, senior high brings a breath of fresh air after the suffocating social environment of middle school. By now the most significant transitions and transformations of puberty are well under way or completed for nearly everyone. Physical attributes and attractiveness are still major concerns, but obvious differences in development among members of this age-group are far less common. While peer influence remains strong, many of the extreme, often ridiculous herd instincts of two or three years ago have begun to fade. No longer does everyone need to look, dress, and talk exactly alike to avoid nonstop ridicule.

Opposite-sex relationships are likely to move beyond crushes and awkward non-conversations into friendships and romances that can displace the same-sex and group camaraderie of the past. The issue of appropriate expressions of physical affection should be broached candidly.

Teens in this age bracket tend to find at least one group they identify with and that provides friendships, fun, and a sense of identity. Church and service organizations, athletics, performing arts (music, drama, dance, film), academics, and even political/ social activism will bring kindred spirits together.

For many families these years bring a crescendo of conflict. In order to demonstrate his separation from your influence, your teen may undergo extreme alterations of appearance, including weird haircuts and hair colors, body piercing, tattoos, and clothing that looks like it came from another planet. If you have a major blowup over some issue, he may take off for parts unknown.

Furthermore, adolescents at this age are capable of carrying out acts with far more serious consequences. Their quest for self-determination or their outright rebellion can be combined and energized by an unspoken belief in their own power and immortality. As a result, risky behavior involving alcohol, drugs, and motor vehicles, as well as other physical feats of daring and stupidity, are more likely now. Intense sexual drives, sensual imagery in films and music, peer pressure, and increased opportunities for intimacy markedly increase the risk for sexual encounters.

For the vast majority of teens, a rebellious phase will eventually end. Only a small percentage will doggedly continue in antisocial and self-destructive paths. Usually a combination of maturing emotions, stabilizing identity, and unpleasant consequences brings an unruly adolescent to his or her senses. As the years pass and the school of life dishes out hard lessons and reality checks, parents seem to gain intelligence in the eyes of their maturing offspring. In a few decades many of today's rebels will be asking their parents for advice about their own teenagers' uprisings.

How do I prepare my late adolescent for independent adulthood?

The conclusion of the teen years and the beginning of the twenties often bring stability to a number of areas but also raise new issues. Concern about physical appearance is rarely the ongoing issue it was during early adolescence, and direct peer-group manipulation of opinions and actions will be less obvious.

Your advice and values will be more readily accepted, acknowledged, or at least tolerated by your older adolescent. While active rebellion is likely to subside as the twenties arrive, some consequences of unwise behavior during the latter teenage years may not go away entirely. But whether the past few years have been smooth sailing or stormy weather, the dawn of independent adult life now looms on the horizon. Your parenting job isn't over until you have escorted your grown child across this threshold into the world of grown-up rights and responsibilities. In a real sense, you will work yourself out of a full-time job.

This process includes a number of transitions that may prove as challenging for you as for your teenager. You must progress from parent to caring friend and confidant; from gravy train to career guide; from being in charge to giving friendly advice—if asked; and from bailing out and mopping up to allowing some consequences to be suffered.

As in all previous parenting tasks, extremes should be avoided. Give a teenager too much independence too early, and she may suffer serious harm in the School of Hard Knocks. But hold the reins too tight for too long, and you may endure one of these equally painful scenarios:

- A strong-willed young adult who literally tears herself out of your sphere of influence, leaving gaping emotional wounds.
- A compliant "good boy" who never learns how to make his own decisions or earn his own way in the world.
- A rebellious and reckless adolescent/young adult who repeatedly gets into hot water and is always promptly bailed out by concerned and caring parents.
- The adult child who hangs out at the happy homestead long after her formal education has come to an end and sees no urgency in seeking her own means of support.

As the adolescent years pass, your teenager needs to hear repeatedly that you will always love her (whatever paths she chooses) but that your parenting role will be coming to an end much sooner than she realizes. Your public-service announcements are as important for the strong-willed fifteen-year-old who is stomping her feet and demanding more freedom ("I'm not a child anymore!") as they are for the laid-back eighteen-year-old who needs to know that the free meal ticket won't be issued forever. The responsibilities you transfer will become more complex—driving a car, balancing a checkbook, and (scariest of all) picking a spouse, among many others. But by walking step-by-step with your adolescent through these processes, your final release will seem like a small step rather than a plunge off a cliff.

How do I teach my teenager adult responsibilities?

As we have said previously, some resistance against limits and contraints—especially those imposed by parents—is a normal (and in fact necessary) part of growing up. You thus have an important job ahead of you during these years: releasing your control over your child who is growing toward adulthood, but doing so in a thoughtful and reasonable way.

Even more important is linking your adolescent's blossoming independence to the realities and responsibilities of adult life. Indeed, teaching your adolescent adult independence and responsibilities is a balancing act. With rare exception teenagers are very eager to have as much of the first and as little of the second as possible. Ideally, they should experience similar amounts of each. Keep in mind that this includes an introduction to many of the mundane tasks you take for granted every week.

Does your daughter want her own car? If you help her obtain one, she needs to be involved in the whole package. What does the registration cost? What about the insurance? How about maintenance? The use of an automobile should rarely be unconditional. Reasonable school performance, trustworthiness, and probably some contribution to expenses (perhaps the insurance, the upkeep, or even saving up for a percentage of the whole purchase) should be part of the bargain. If she gets a ticket, she's going to have to pay for it. Let her look over the registration bill every year as well. This isn't much fun, but she'll have to do it eventually when she's out of the nest.

Another useful reality check is escorting your teenager on a guided tour of your monthly bills. Let your son see what you pay for mortgage, taxes, utilities, and the other things he takes for granted every month. Better yet, let him fill out the checks and the register with you during a bill-paying session. He'll learn about a few significant nuts and bolts of everyday life and save you some time as well. Help him open his own checking account, and show him how to balance it every month.

It also should go without saying that every member of the household should have specified duties in maintaining cleanliness and order. Be sure to hand out age-appropriate housekeeping assignments (which may be daily, weekly, or both), with the understanding that the children should do their chores automatically without requiring nonstop nagging and reminders. If you hear whining about this being an imposition, slave labor, etc., remind the complainer that this is merely the way civilized, responsible grown-ups live.

If your adolescent's behavior causes any harm or damage, whether accidental or otherwise, make sure she participates in the restitution and repairs. If you automatically bail her out of every consequence, you will succeed only in perpetuating childish irresponsibility. Indeed, one of the most significant parting gifts you can provide for a grown child is a practical, working knowledge of consequences. Adulthood often involves asking sober questions about a future course of action: "If I do _____, what is likely to happen? What things might go wrong with my plans? What do I need to do to prepare for the possibilities?"

When your teen has a red-hot idea for an activity or a project, enjoy her enthusiasm but also coach her through the potential problems she may not have thought about. At times she may think you're a party pooper for bringing up the negatives, but reassure her that you're only doing so because she's almost an adult—and that's what adults do.

How can I be a positive influence on my child?

The foundation for influencing your teen (in the right direction) is building your relationship with him. Show genuine interest and respect. Teens despise being treated like little kids. They hate being talked down to. They bristle when orders are dished out and there's no room for discussion. If they try to express a heart-felt thought and no one listens or someone ridicules it, they shut down. More often than not, their tempers flare and their feelings are hurt because of the *way* something is said—disrespectfully—rather than because of the actual issue.

In other words, they are just like adults.

Even though your teenager may be light-years away from grown-up maturity and responsibilities, you will build strong bonds and smooth your mutual pathway over the next few years by talking to him as you would to another adult you respect. This, like anything else in life that is worthwhile, takes time and energy. Specific ways to build and maintain a relationship with your teen-ager include the following:

- *Take her out for a meal, one-on-one, on a regular basis*—monthly at least, and more often if possible. Ask questions about what she's interested in, and listen carefully to what she says. The cuisine doesn't have to be expensive. What you're buying is more than food—it's undistracted, uninter-rupted time to find out what your adolescent is thinking about. (You don't need to wait until the teen years to start this tradition, by the way.) For extra credit, stroll with her through her favorite mall or other shopping destination. Pay attention to what she likes, and you'll always have plenty of ideas for birthday or Christmas gifts.
- *Take advantage of common interests.* Does he love to ski? Take some time off work and head for the nearest mountain that has snow and ski trails on it. Is he an avid movie- or

theatergoer? Go with him and talk about what you've seen. Is he crazy about baseball or softball? Go out to a ball game together, and be sure to show up to watch if he is on a team. Does he enjoy chess, Scrabble, or other games? Become a willing (but not too aggressive) opponent.

- *Ask your teen's opinions about things going on in the world, your community, and your family.* If she says something that isn't exactly well-informed, don't jump in and "straighten her out." You can gently guide teenagers in the right direction during the natural flow of conversation without making them feel stupid after opening up about their views. When your teen wants to talk, stop what you're doing, establish eye contact, and pay attention.

- *Find things to praise and do it often*—even when there's always much more that you might criticize. Like anyone else, teenagers respond well to encouragement.

- *Have the courage to apologize.* If you commit a genuine offense—whether it's a sarcastic or hurtful comment or an action that causes your teenager embarrassment or pain—or some other error in judgment, be the first to admit you were wrong. You will not lose face by doing so—instead you will gain great respect (though you may not hear about it until a few years have passed).

- *Express satisfaction or outright joy that your daughter or son is yours.* If you have trouble with this, ask yourself why. It could be that you are breaking new ground here, modeling unconditional acceptance that you didn't feel when you were growing up.

How can I encourage a proper body image in my child?

Teens are keenly interested, and at times seemingly obsessed, with body image—both their own and everyone else's. As a result, they are constantly comparing themselves with others. Whoever holds the winning ticket in the appearance sweepstakes—the most attractive features, the knockout figure, the well-sculpted muscles, the athletic prowess—will nearly always reign supreme whenever teens gather. But even those who seem destined to appear on the cover of *People* magazine struggle with doubts about their appearance and worth.

No matter how well assembled your teenager might appear to you and others, from his own perspective someone will always have a better package. Negative comparisons—sometimes amazingly unrealistic ones—are likely. And an adolescent with an obvious physical deficit may be cruelly taunted by peers and develop a lifelong preoccupation with appearance. Accepting one's body and taking appropriate care of it are important tasks to be accomplished during the transition to adulthood.

Your job here is a delicate one. Your teenager will need generous doses of reassurance that worth does not depend on appearance, even when the surrounding culture says otherwise. You will have to endure the fact that any positive comments you make about looks, temperament, accomplishments, or inherent value may not be met with expressions of thanks. It may appear that what you say doesn't count, but it does—in a big way.

One challenge for parents is to find the fine line between making constructive suggestions and being a nag. Your adolescent's preoccupation with looks may not necessarily translate into specific actions to improve them or to appear pleasing to adults. In fact, at times the opposite will be true. The current "dress code" at middle school, for example, may decree an extremely casual, semi-unkempt look in order to appear "normal." Within limits, generational differences in clothing and hairstyle may not be worth a family battle.

But sometimes you may need to take the initiative. If your son suffers from acne, he'll need your help and some professional input to bring the blemishes under control. If your daughter is clueless about clothes, you or a savvy relative may need to help rehabilitate the wardrobe (which does not need to be an expensive project). If weight is a problem, tactful efforts to move the scale in the right direction may improve your adolescent's self-image and general health. These efforts should be positive, emphasizing healthy foods and activities for everyone in the family without focusing attention on one person. If your teen has a major problem with food—whether an unhealthy obsession with thinness, or weight that is far above the norm—professional help should be sought from a physician, dietitian, counselor, or all of the above. (See the questions on eating disorders in chapter 6.)

Whether or not teens are comfortable with their physical appearance, they must decide how they will care for themselves. Lifestyle and habits established at this age may continue well into adulthood, and it is never too early to establish a healthy respect for one's body. Prudent eating habits can be modeled and encouraged, and you can also point out that exercise isn't merely something to be endured during PE class, but is also worth pursuing (in moderation) for its own sake. Unfortunately, some teenagers who harbor a mistaken belief that "nothing bad can happen to me" choose to engage in substance abuse, sexual misadventures, and other risk-taking behaviors that could establish long-standing negative habits or leave permanent physical (not to mention emotional) scars.

Most likely, you established the roots of a healthy self-image in your child during the preschool years. Even so, reasonable vigilance, good role modeling, and forthright and open conversations about risky behavior will need to be on your agenda until your adolescent has completed the transition to full independence.

How can I help my child develop a healthy sense of identity?

Whether they are National Merit Scholars or total nonconformists (or both), teens are fervently searching for a clear sense of identity. Whatever the guise or getup, the questions they ask boil down to two: *Who cares about me?* and *What can I do that has significance?*

If the answers are "God, my family, and my close friends" and "have a positive impact on the world," your main task—and it usually will be a pleasant one—will be serving as cheerleader and sounding board as your son or daughter finds the best track on which to run.

If the answers are "my friends (and hardly anyone else)" and "have fun (and hardly anything else)," the ultimate outcome could be more unpredictable. Though most teens with this mind-set eventually grow up and find a productive niche, some may stay in this shallow, meandering rut well into adulthood. Some may also drift into drug use or sexual activity in their search for the next diversion—and ultimately pay dearly for it. (See chapter 4 on teen sexuality and chapter 5 on drug use.)

For the teenager whose answers are "no one" and "nothing," if different answers are nowhere on the horizon, the consequences may be more serious: depression, acting out, even suicidal behavior. (See the questions on depression starting on page 166).

Obviously, it is important that your child enter adolescence with some clear and positive answers to the questions of caring and significance. During the coming seasons, he will probably ask them often and in many different ways—some of which may catch you off guard. Even if he has lost his bearings or abandoned common sense, you will still need to communicate that your love and his significance are unshakable. As in earlier years of childhood, you will need to enforce limits and help him make some course corrections until he is on his own. But he must always know that your fundamental love for him will never change, regardless of grades, clothes, a messy room, dented fenders, or more serious issues.

How can I encourage a positive worldview?

The adolescent years are a crucial period in an individual's development of a worldview—the basic (and often unspoken) assumptions that govern attitudes, decisions, and actions. Young people often make decisions during their teen years that will set a course for the rest of their lives. Many make permanent spiritual commitments at church, camp, or other events and continue to mature in their faith as the years pass. But these are also years during which fundamental questions about God and the universe are asked, and parents may find their own beliefs (or lack thereof) held up for inspection.

Many teens feel the need to chart a different spiritual course from that of their parents during these years, a development that can make parents feel very uneasy. *What if she turns away from God and all we have taught her over the years?* Before you lose too much sleep over this question, remember that your child must eventually make her own decision whether or not to follow God. You can't do it for her. In fact, it's healthy for her to examine what she has learned as a child because eventually she must understand how her faith applies to adult situations and problems.

Your primary job will be to keep your *own* relationship with God thriving—which should include meaningful time in prayer for your child on an ongoing basis. Spiritual vitality that consistently manifests genuine joy, peace, and other positive expressions will ultimately communicate more to your adolescent than a lot of clever (or convoluted) answers to her questions. In matters of faith (and in other arenas as well), teenagers are particularly responsive to honesty and integrity and turned off with equal fervor by hypocrisy.

If her need to assert her independence from you spills into the spiritual realm, you may need to entrust her growth in this area to other adults (or even peers) who can positively influence her view of God, faith, and the world in general. Youth leaders, teachers, young couples or single adults, or other friends of the family can often "stand in the gap" for you in this area. Do what you can to encourage these contacts and interactions (without being pushy about it) and then leave the results in God's hands.

How can I encourage my teenager to accept people who are different?

Helping our children develop a positive worldview also involves shaping their view of people who hold different positions—or for that matter, are different in any number of other ways. They need to know when and how to stand their ground when the values they care about are challenged. In our relativistic culture, holding a solid position on almost anything (especially in the realm of spirituality or sexuality) is often ridiculed or condemned as intolerant. Caving in to that view, or going to the opposite extreme and attacking those who think differently, should be strongly discouraged. A critical skill to teach is that of expressing one's viewpoints clearly to others, whatever their belief systems, while treating them with utmost respect. (Assuming your son or daughter marries, he or she will benefit from this capability when conflict arises with a spouse.)

Respect for the rights and feelings of others applies to a much bigger relational canvas, by the way. It is important not only when discussing opinions, but also when encountering anyone who is different in some way: skin color, ethnic background, accent, native language, shape and size, disabilities, emotional quirks, age, appearance, you name it. What's the best way to teach respect (or its evil counterparts, disrespect, prejudice, and abuse)? Far and away, what you model will speak the loudest. Say all you want about the importance of being kind to others, but what your kids see and hear will have the greater impact.

How can I encourage my child's gifts and abilities?

One of the most important and life-enhancing aspects of adolescence is the process of looking at a variety of activities and interests. If childhood interests in soccer or piano-playing, for example, don't continue into the teen years, don't count your time spent in those activities as wasted. Your teen may want to explore drama or gymnastics for a while, and they may become her new passions—or she may discover that the piano really is her true love after all. Your encouragement to find and develop her strengths, and perhaps to overcome what she (and you) might consider her weaknesses, will pay off in many ways. Not only might she find a niche of true excellence and accomplishment, but all of these activities—even the ones that don't pan out as permanent interests—will broaden her fund of knowledge and experience. Furthermore, your support during these efforts will repeatedly affirm her value.

This is also a time during which many young people develop and hone a social conscience. Altruism often peaks during the teen years, and your teenager may find considerable satisfaction in helping others solve problems and in volunteering to serve in worthy causes. Teenagers can be surprisingly empathetic to the suffering of others, and they may go to great lengths of energy and time to lend someone a helping hand. You will obviously want to encourage selfless and sacrificial behavior—in fact, at times, you may find your own conscience stirred by your adolescent's willingness to love the unlovely.

In addition, many states and school districts require a student to complete a certain number of hours of community service in order to graduate, and colleges may also look for participation in a variety of nonacademic activities—including service projects—as they evaluate applicants. In some ways this idea of "mandatory" service may seem paradoxical—*If this is supposed to be volunteer work, why am I required to do it?*—but navigating through this assignment can be a golden opportunity for a number of worthwhile discussions. For example, helping people who lack basic resources can be eye-opening for a teenager whose material needs have been consistently met at home. Learning that "it's not always about you" through serving others is a big step toward growing up and succeeding in education, work, marriage, and parenting, not to mention gaining spiritual maturity.

You should model practical concern for the needs of others while at the same time guiding the parameters of your teen's involvement. For example, your daughter might want to rescue a friend from an abusive family situation by inviting her to stay at your home. Perhaps you are able to offer a safe haven—certainly an honorable and meaningful action—but you will also need to walk your daughter through some of the realities and details that may not have occurred to her in the rush to help. If you have a particularly generous and tenderhearted teen at home, you will have to pass along a little street wisdom to prevent her charitable instincts from becoming soured by encounters with users and abusers who might take advantage of her.

How can I encourage healthy peer relationships?

The impact of peers on teens cannot be underestimated. The right people crossing their paths at critical times can reinforce positive values and enhance the entire process of growing up. The wrong individuals can escort them into extremely negative detours or suck the life out of them.

Because peers can play such a serious role for good or ill in your teen's life, you will need to be forthright and intentional about where, and with whom, time is spent—especially in the early years. If the drama club, 4-H, or athletic teams provide a consistently healthy niche, by all means encourage them. But if a new "friend" who manifests an abundance of toxic language and behavior enters your adolescent's life, don't hesitate to take some defensive measures. This may include insisting that they spend time together only under your roof with an adult on the premises (and no closed bedroom doors). If it becomes apparent that your teenager is being swayed toward destructive habits, however, reasonable measures to separate him from negative influences will be necessary.

If your church has a strong and active youth group, do everything you can to support it and your teen's involvement in it. But if your youth group has gone stale or has become a clique zone, find another one. The program should honor your family's faith and values, of course, but should also accept all comers, build positive identities, and be fun as it promotes spiritual growth.

Your job is to pray with utter abandon for the friends your adolescent will make over the next several years. Without being too pushy about it, make every effort to make friends with your teenager's friends. If your home is the most teen friendly in the neighborhood, chances are the troops will gather under your roof or in your backyard and respond to your influence in the process.

As much as you can, get to know and even make friends with your teenager's friends. Listen to what they have to say. An adolescent who likes and respects you will be less likely to encourage your teenager to disregard your opinions. You may be able to smooth out a conflict between one of your teen's friends and her parents. You might even learn a thing or two about your own child. As you get to know your teen's friends, you can also pray for them.

If you can't connect and it appears that one or more friends are pulling your teenager in directions that are destructive or dangerous, you may have to take the social bull by the horns. Calmly, rationally, and carefully present your concerns. Very often, your teenager may be relieved to have a reason to disengage from one or more relationships. In a *worst-case* scenario, you may have to insist that one or more friends are off-limits, which will probably generate a fair amount of protest. Obviously, you can't patrol the corridors at school, but you need to make it clear that freedom and privileges will be seriously restricted if your teenager refuses to cooperate. Keep in mind that this plan of action should be reserved for situations in which your child's health and welfare

are clearly on the line—not for isolating your teenager from friends whom you merely find annoying.

What should I do if I disagree with a teacher or with the curriculum used at my child's school?

It goes without saying that your teenager's schoolwork should include the basics: reading, writing, math, history, and so forth. In general, it's reasonable to assume your local schools are staffed by men and women who take their jobs seriously and have their students' best interests at heart.

But what if a particular teacher seems to have it in for your son or daughter, or a class appears to be pushing a political or social agenda that disagrees with yours? What if the family life or sex education unit contradicts the basic values you teach at home? More important, what if your adolescent is subjected to ridicule for expressing a contrary point of view?

Once again, a calm but purposeful approach is in order. You shouldn't abandon your teenager to fend completely for himself. But you should avoid charging into any situation at school with righteous indignation and verbal guns blazing.

First, get all the facts. Find out what "My teacher doesn't like me!" really means. What exactly was said? Is there a pattern? Can you get some written material from the class to look at? Is it possible that your teenager is primarily at fault because of disrespectful or inattentive behavior? It may help to talk to someone else in the same class to get confirmation that a problem really does exist.

You may be able to coach your adolescent through the situation by suggesting ways to de-escalate a conflict (including apologizing, if necessary). If the problem involves a clash of viewpoints, it may in fact be character building for your teenager to deal with differences of opinion in an open forum. In this case, you may choose to help him review the facts to bolster his viewpoint or find someone who can provide the input he needs. Remember—it won't hurt him to think through and defend what he believes.

Think carefully before you demand or choose to have your son or daughter opt out of a controversial activity. This may seem a noble gesture on your part, but it might generate a lot of unnecessary ridicule from peers. For example, if a teacher or speaker gives a skewed presentation on sexual behavior (emphasizing condom use over abstinence), it may be appropriate for your teen to hear it—and then have an open discussion and review at home afterward. This may also be a starting point for you to influence the future curriculum in a more positive direction. On the other hand, if you have advance warning that extremely offensive material is going to be used, exercise the opt-out choice—and then work diligently to change what happens next year.

If it looks as if the situation is out of hand (for example, your teenager is obviously upset, developing physical symptoms, or doesn't want to go to school because of the pressure) or the deck is stacked (points and grades in the class appear to depend on agreement with a teacher's ideology), you'll need to enter the arena.

Schedule an appointment with the teacher to get his perspective on the situation. Ask an open question: "Teresa seems to be having some problems in your class. What can we do to smooth things out?" If you begin with "Why are you picking on my daughter?" or "You're out of line, and I'm taking this all the way to the school board!" there won't be any discussion at all.

Perhaps you haven't gotten the whole story. Maybe some evenhanded give-and-take on controversial issues has been encouraged, and your teenager didn't present her views very well. If so, building bridges rather than lighting fires would be a better course of action.

If, however, it is clear that certain beliefs and viewpoints aren't welcome or are subject to ridicule in the class, and friendly persuasion isn't making any headway, you may have to pursue your teenager's right to a hassle-free education. A meeting of other like-minded parents with the teacher in question, a conference with the principal, or a transfer to another class may be appropriate. Your bottom line should not be a tirade that "This school is leading our youth down the road to ruin," but rather the simple notion that school should be a neutral ground for mastering basic material, not pushing a specific social or political agenda.

What is the importance of opposite-gender parental relationships?

In many families, fathers have more interests in common with their sons, and mothers with their daughters. But the importance of nurturing father-daughter and mother-son relationships cannot be overstated.

The tendency in father-son and mother-daughter relationships is for the parent to compare (with some anxiety) the progress of the child to memories of his own adolescence. Thoughts such as *He's not doing as well as I was at this age* or *I don't want her to make the same mistakes I did while growing up* can cloud your appreciation of your teenager's uniqueness and your enjoyment of his company. Because Dad was never a girl and Mom was never a boy, these ongoing comparisons and concerns aren't as likely in opposite-gender relationships.

A girl's father is usually the man in her life for many years. How he treats her will affect her relationships with other men throughout her teenage and adult years. She will look to him for affection, respect, and affirmation of her femininity and will usually expect the same type of treatment from the males in her life later on. If she has lived with neglect, criticism, and abuse, she may spend years enduring the same from men who are self-centered, irresponsible, and predatory. But if she has been treated with courtesy and respect by her father, she isn't likely to tolerate men who treat her otherwise.

For a variety of reasons, mothers and daughters may butt

heads more often during the adolescent years than at other times in their lives. A father's input can help de-escalate conflicts and build Mom's image in the mind of his frustrated daughter.

Mothers can also have a unique relationship with their teenage sons. Though Dad should teach his sons the proper way to treat members of the opposite sex, Mom can usually serve as an adviser regarding matters of the heart. If a son is struggling with a relationship that is tying his emotions in knots, a woman's perspective can offer both insight and comfort.

How should I manage conflict with my teenager?

Differences of opinion with a growing adolescent on a variety of subjects are inevitable. Even a teenager who is compliant and agreeable will lock horns with you eventually—or become an expert at quieter ways of rebellion. When you are challenged on a rule at home, or you see or hear your teenager doing something you don't like, a few basic principles can help.

"Do not exasperate your children" (Ephesians 6:4). If you choose to comment, nag, or nudge about everything your teenager does that isn't up to your standards, be prepared for several years of misery. Yes, she needs your guidance. The choices she makes now can have significant consequences, and she still has lots of room for improvement. But if she constantly hears about her deficits, she will become frustrated and eventually hostile. And guess who she won't want to talk to if there's a *real* problem? If all the nitpicky stuff arouses nonstop criticism at home, how can she expect a measured response to a major mistake?

Think through your rules. Ask yourself regularly, "Why am I making this rule?" Does it truly affect your adolescent's well-being? Or does it merely reflect the way things were done when you were growing up?

Don't be afraid to negotiate in some areas. If your teenager respectfully suggests an alternative to a rule or restriction you've imposed, listen carefully. If it's reasonable, seriously consider letting the decision go his way. You will gain some major points and demonstrate that you are truly listening rather than merely reacting.

Go to the mat when necessary. Issues regarding health, safety, moral principles, or attitudes will require you to state your case and hold your ground. You must still be friendly. You can discuss the reasons and suggest alternatives. You can remind your teenager that his independence is not too many years away, but for now you're still in charge in a few key areas. You must reinforce your love for him and treat him with respect. But even though you may risk a temporary decline in popularity, when it's time to take a stand, don't shirk your duty.

What if my teen absolutely rebels against my authority?

If you find yourself embroiled in a civil war at home or confronted by a teenager who is making some dangerously bad decisions, you need to keep these principles in mind:

Take the bull by the horns. Don't tolerate flagrant disrespect, destruction of your home or other property, criminal activity, or abuse from your teenager. Drastic action may be necessary to keep this type of behavior from tearing your family to shreds. You may need to enlist help from a number of allies, including other parents, counselors, your pastor, your adolescent's physician, and the police. If more conservative measures aren't working, you may need to consider informing her that she cannot remain under your roof if these acts continue. Living at home then becomes a privilege to be earned on your terms, with some critical minimum requirements: no drugs, no booze, no stealing, no sex, and no verbal or physical abuse of anyone in the family.

And that's just the beginning. Most states require that parents supply their children younger than eighteen with the following necessities: food, shelter, a mattress on the floor, two changes of clothes, and medical care. Everything else is optional and can be considered additional privileges to be earned by appropriate behavior. A car, phone, iPod, computer, closet full of clothes, decorations on the wall, even the door to the room are privileges that can be removed from a minor's possession until further notice. This may sound harsh, but too many parents who wring their hands over their teenager's wild behavior are also paying all of the prodigal's bills. Cutting the supply line for a while can be an effective way to restore order. If at all possible, it would be wise to work with a counselor who is experienced in adolescent issues (and who knows your state's laws regarding the "bare necessities" you must provide) when taking decisive steps like these.

If she breaks the law and is arrested, depending on the circumstances you may need to choose not to bail her out, as painful as this decision would be. In doing so you would have but one purpose: allowing her to experience the brunt of her bad decisions and to come to her senses.

Don't live with false guilt. Perhaps you have made mistakes (who hasn't?) in raising your prodigal offspring. But even those who work diligently to "train a child in the way he should go" (Proverbs 22:6) can find themselves in the midst of a parent's nightmare. Each child is an independent being with a free will who decides if he will proceed "in the way he should go" or "depart from it." Even this famous verse is not an ironclad guarantee but a statement of the way things generally happen.

Don't underestimate the depth of your adolescent's emotions.
Serious problems are not "just a phase she's going through," and
often disruptive behavior on a child's part is the manifestation
of real suffering and inner turmoil. Sometimes serious emotional
and behavioral issues arise from conditions with underlying biochemical disturbances that are responsive to medical treatment
(including anxiety disorders, depression, bipolar disorder, and
even schizophrenia). By all means seek professional help, including psychiatric consultation if necessary.

Pray without ceasing, and don't give up. Even if you have to
allow your child to reap the bitter harvest of his choices, continue
praying for his safety and return to sanity. More often than not,
even the most die-hard prodigals eventually get tired of the pigsty
and trudge home.

What is and isn't worth a battle?

Some things that bother you may not be worth a major conflict
with your teenager. Think carefully before starting a war over

- a messy room (unless the health department pays a visit);
- length of hair;
- earrings (for either gender);
- style of music;
- sound level of music;
- choice of everyday clothing;
- fast food;
- sleeping in when there's not a specific need to arise for
  school or work; or
- how, when, and where homework is done—as long as it is
  getting done.

On the other hand, there are a number of areas (some related to the list above) in which you will need to state your case and hold your ground, or at least have some family summit conferences to resolve your differences:

A mess not confined to her room. If you are constantly gathering up your teenager's stuff from every room, it's time for retraining. Let everyone know that you have resigned from unpaid janitorial duties. Furthermore, after one or two reminders, valuables will be confiscated for an unspecified period, and undisposed trash may end up in the teenager's bed. You can declare your intentions humorously, of course, but be sure to follow through.

Extreme alterations of hair. A heart-to-heart talk is in order if your adolescent plans to adopt a totally bizarre hairstyle (such as giant green spikes) that will blatantly announce to the world, "I don't care what anybody thinks of me!" Important issues of acceptance and rejection lie below the surface of outlaw or alien appearances and deserve thoughtful exploration rather than ridicule.

Tattoos. Despite a rising acceptance of "body art" in many circles, your adolescent needs to know that it is extremely unwise to do *anything* with permanent physical consequences when his life is in a state of flux. This is particularly important if he seems intent on embedding negative or offensive images in his skin. It will cost him a lot of money and discomfort if he wants them removed later on, which is likely. He should also be aware that serious viral infections such as hepatitis B, hepatitis C, or HIV, as well as bacterial skin infections, can be spread by contaminated tattoo needles. A makeshift "tattoo parlor" in a friend's garage should be avoided at all costs. Tell him he can have all the tattoos he wants—after he is eighteen and living on his own. By then his interest in body alterations may well have passed.

Body piercing. Aggressive body piercing (nose, tongue, navel, etc.) should be discouraged, perhaps with a reminder about respecting one's body and resisting peer pressure. As with tattoos, serious viral infections can be spread if contaminated instruments are used during piercing. In addition, if a bacterial infection arises around any embedded hardware, it will need to be removed—a process that can be quite uncomfortable.

Sound level of music. If your adolescent's music is keeping everyone at home (or the entire neighborhood) awake at night, or if you can hear it across the room when he's wearing headphones or earbuds, you will need to insist that the volume come down. Ongoing exposure to extremely loud noise can cause permanent hearing loss.

Choice of everyday clothing. If garments contain images or words that are violent or offensive, they don't belong on your adolescent. You will also need to veto female attire that is blatantly sexually provocative. Remind your child of any school policies regarding clothing to be worn on campus.

Extremes in food choices—either excessive or limited in variety or amount. Obesity in adolescence is not only a social issue, but may also set in motion lifelong health problems. Anorexia and bulimia are obsessions with food that can have very serious consequences as well. (See the questions on eating disorders in chapter 6.) Both undereating and overeating deserve focused attention and help from your health-care provider, a dietitian, and a counselor who is experienced with these issues. Anorexia may require psychiatric hospitalization because it can be very difficult to treat.

Disappearing. In any home, it is a common courtesy—and may be critically important in an emergency—for family members who live under the same roof to be notified of each other's whereabouts. Your teenager needs to understand that this doesn't mean you're treating her like a child. It is childish and irresponsible to take off for hours at a time—especially at night—without keeping the home front posted. Remind her that this expectation applies to everyone in your home, parents included. If she's going to be at a friend's house for the evening, it's not unreasonable for you to get a name and number. If she's going to go somewhere else, you need to know the destination.

As your teenager progresses through high school, let her know that you intend to give her more latitude about the time she is expected home if she is trustworthy in this area.

Disrespectful comments and actions. If you find yourself on the receiving end of sarcastic or abusive language—or if you hear it being dished out to others in the home—you need to end the conversation immediately. Calmly explain that the issue is no longer whatever was being discussed, but the unacceptable way in which the ideas were expressed. You may get a blank stare, and you may need to spell out what you found objectionable. If your teenager responds appropriately, the conversation can proceed—and you will have provided an object lesson for your adolescent in how to handle issues later in life.

If your teenager will not back away from the inappropriate comments, or if the problem escalates, more drastic action will be necessary. You may need to enlist the help of a professional counselor who shares your basic values.

How can I prepare my teen to be a responsible driver?

Driving is one of the most momentous steps a teenager will take toward personal independence. Being able to drive provides mobility, the gratification of not having to rely on parents or friends for a ride, and a definite sense of prestige (even if the vehicle involved is the family fixer-upper). As with every other new freedom that beckons the adolescent moving toward adulthood, a number of risks—and responsibilities—must be acknowledged and addressed. Because of the safety issues that accompany taking the wheel for the first time, new drivers and their parents should prepare for this next phase of life with the utmost diligence.

If you're apprehensive about your teenager becoming a driver, your concerns are not unfounded. Inexperience is a major risk factor for teens involved in accidents. Driving is, after all, an amazingly complex task. New drivers must learn to control their vehicle and its speed, while at the same time detecting and responding to hazardous driving conditions and emergency situations. The vast majority of teens are not lacking in the motor skills and coordination necessary to be excellent drivers—they're probably better equipped in this regard than Mom and Dad—but what isn't fully developed yet is their judgment (experience-based decision-making ability) or a healthy respect for the unexpected—and their own mortality.

Indeed, an important factor contributing to accidents involving teens is their willingness to engage in risky behaviors. Speeding, driving under the influence of alcohol or drugs, using cell phones or texting while driving, talking with friends in the car, and not always buckling their seat belts are factors in many traffic accidents and fatalities involving teenagers.

After reading the grim statistics on teenage injuries or fatalities resulting from automobile accidents—see http://www.nhtsa.gov /Teen-Drivers, for example, if you want a sobering reality check— some parents may vow not to let their children get behind the wheel of a car until they are in their twenties and living on their own. Aside from being unrealistic, such a mind-set is counterproductive and insulting to teens who really want to learn to drive safely. A more constructive outlook is to view the adolescent years as a time when adults can teach safe driving habits and influence a young driver's behavior for life, imparting skills and knowledge that will perhaps save lives many years in the future. Becoming an expert driver requires years of experience. Overseeing the first few years of that experience is a wonderful, though at times ulcer-generating, privilege.

What are some rules I can implement as my teen learns to drive?

As a parent, you can pass on a wealth of driving wisdom in many ways. First, be patient with your teen. His learning to drive may be nerve-racking for you, but it's much more so for him. (Giving all instructions calmly and clearly will help.) Second, as with other good behaviors parents want their children to adopt, you must model safe driving habits. For better or worse, children will imitate their parents. Also, parents should not only learn the teenage driving laws for their state, but also be prepared to enforce additional limits and expectations based on their adolescent's attitude and skill.

Recognizing that driver-education courses by themselves are not a complete preparation for novice motorists, nearly every state has instituted graduated licensing for teens. Such a system is designed to phase teens into full driving privileges by allowing them to mature and develop their driving skills in stages. Each state's system is different, but the typical graduated-licensing model involves three stages. Beginners must remain in the first two stages for a minimum amount of time, demonstrating a mastery of basic skills under less-challenging driving conditions. For example, the stage-one teenage driver might not be allowed to drive after dark, while in stage two he might be allowed to drive at night, but only with adult supervision. (To check on your state's requirements for teen drivers, visit the Governors Highway

Safety Association website at www.ghsa.org/html/stateinfo/laws /license_laws.html.)

Even if your state has not yet enacted graduated licensing, you may wish to grant your teen's driving privileges in a similar manner, which allows him to acquire the experience he needs while reducing some of the risks. For example, you might require that your teen driver be accompanied by a parent or other responsible licensed adult driver at all times for a set period of time. You may also wish to set specific ground rules, such as limiting the number of passengers he may have in the car or restricting driving to daylight hours, until he has demonstrated responsible driving behavior for a number of weeks or months.

Always require your teen to buckle up before the engine is started, whether driving or riding. (This is an area where your example speaks louder than your words.) Your adolescent should never drive if he is drowsy. Additionally, though there are many good reasons for him to abstain from alcohol and drugs, don't fail to drive home the message that drinking kills thousands of people every year—many of them teens. Not only should your teenager never drink and drive, but he should also never get into a car if the driver has been drinking. No matter how strongly you may feel about the use of alcohol, let your adolescent know that he can *always* call you for a ride in order to avoid being in a car with an intoxicated driver—whether himself or someone else.

Remind your teenager that in most states, texting while driving is illegal. (You might add that it's an incredibly bad idea in all fifty states.) You should also caution your budding driver against answering the phone or talking on it while driving. Most states ban *any* cell phone use by novice drivers. (You can check your state's laws at http://www.ghsa.org. Click on "Cell Phone and Texting Laws.") Though many people try to multitask, few are able to do so safely. Inexperienced drivers are asking for trouble when they add another distraction to their driving.

Unfortunately, no matter how calmly and rationally you explain the conditions you are placing on your teen, he may see these restrictions as unreasonable. If he protests your limitations, stand your ground. And if you see unsafe driving patterns or habits that your adolescent refuses to correct, don't let him have the keys. The first commandment for would-be drivers to learn (and burn deep in their consciousness) is that driving is a privilege, not a right. Your first priority is not to win a popularity contest. It's to keep him (and others on the road) alive and well while he learns to operate an automobile safely and skillfully.

CHAPTER 3

TECH SUPPORT: MEDIA, INTERNET, AND MORE

Discretion will protect you,
    and understanding will guard you.

PROVERBS 2:11

ELECTRONIC DEVICES THAT generate sounds and images, or move them from one place and person to another, change so rapidly that keeping up with them can feel like a full-time job. With rare exception, however, your kids are definitely keeping up, whether you like it or not. In fact, at times it may seem as if they are permanently staring at a screen or plugged in to something that's pushing music into their ears a little harder than you'd like.

The pace of new developments in this realm is explosive, and each breakthrough brings great promise for good and potential for harm. At times, you may be tempted to unplug everything and go back to the "good old days," whatever time that was. (In fact, a power failure can sometimes give everyone an eye-opening experience in the pleasures of conversation and reading by candlelight.)

But as a wise parent you can't afford to ignore what's out there or leave your teenagers to their own devices, so to speak. When it comes to media and electronics (like anything else in their world), your kids need your input, guidance, and a lot of conversations about what's wise and what isn't.

What if I don't like the music my child wants to listen to?

With a few exceptions, contemporary music plays a prominent and intense role in the lives and thought processes of teens; this has been true for generations. Today, however, this is not particularly good news.

Pop music runs the gamut from upbeat and even thoughtful (though often mixed with a fair amount of flexible morality) to vivid expressions of obscenity, brutal violence (including rape), sexual anarchy, death, and despair. In between lies a lot of angst, heartache, and emotional turbulence. In bygone days, rebellion was at least supposed to be fun. Now it's often glum or even murderous. Sophisticated videos that accompany rock hits often add a visual punch to the audio assault.

A "Parental Advisory" label is designed to alert adults that a CD or download contains "strong language or depictions of violence, sex, or substance abuse," and that "parental discretion is advised." How effectively it limits access of this material to adolescent ears and minds is debatable. The program is entirely voluntary: The Parental Advisory label is affixed to the product at the discretion of the artist and the company releasing the recording.

Some companies release edited versions of recordings that have been given Parental Advisory labels. These display an "Edited" notice that indicates the content has been toned down, though with no guarantee that it is entirely family friendly. Certain stores—Wal-Mart and Sam's Club are notable examples—will not carry recordings with Parental Advisory labels, though they may sell certain edited editions. Others will not sell Parental Advisory–labeled CDs to anyone under eighteen. But where there's an adolescent will there's a technological way, and if a teenager really wants to hear the latest output from his favorite artist (whose name alone might raise a few eyebrows), virtually anything can be downloaded from the Internet or swapped among friends. (For more information on Parental Advisory labels, you can go to http://riaa.com and click on "Resources." Keep in mind that this is a recording industry website.)

Depending on your teenager's musical tastes, at some point you and he may need to face the music, so to speak. There is simply no way that relentlessly negative and destructive lyrics can pound into a person's mind without making an impact. The issue, by the way, is *content*, not style. Some music that is grating to your ears may actually contain lyrics that challenge the listener to a better lifestyle or tell a cautionary tale.

If you hear something questionable leaking through earbuds or headphones, call for a joint listening session. Get the liner notes, if possible (and a magnifying glass to read them), or download the lyrics from the Internet, and then review the music together with your teenager. Talk about what the lyrics are saying and how he feels when he listens to them. You may hear an argument such as, "I just like the beat and the music. I don't listen to the words." Don't buy it. More often than not, he can recite the lyrics from memory.

You'll need courage to separate your adolescent from music that is toxic, an open mind to endure the stuff that isn't, and wisdom to know the difference. You should also be prepared to suggest alternatives. For families with Christian commitments, there is a thriving world of contemporary music available in a breadth of styles—including pop, rock, rap, metal, and alternative—that specifically (if noisily) promotes positive values. In addition, a little research will uncover secular music that, while not including overtly biblical phrases or themes, combines high-quality musicianship with family friendly themes. Parents who want to stay abreast of the music scene without directly wading through it should consider checking out *Plugged In*, an informative website and e-newsletter that analyzes current offerings with particular attention to content and values (or lack thereof). This resource from Focus on the Family features an extensive Internet archive of music reviews. You can access *Plugged In* at www.pluggedin.com.

How much choice in movies, TV shows, or other media should I allow my teen?

As your teenager grows older, you will need to reassess your ground rules for managing these media. You still have a responsibility to oversee the viewing choices in your home, but you may not be able to govern what she watches at a friend's house. Ideally, ongoing conversations about the content of films and TV programs have already instilled some standards and accountability. If you've nurtured a healthy regard for quality and values, she will feel uneasy if she is exposed to trash and stupidity.

Conflicts may arise when "everyone" has seen a certain R-rated film, and she wants to go too (at the ripe age of fourteen) or watch it on DVD, Blu-ray, cable, or a computer download. You will need to set and maintain your own family's standards, but at some point you may want to introduce your teenager to more grown-up subject matter under your supervision. Do some homework and read the write-ups (especially in family-oriented magazines). Sometimes an otherwise excellent film receives an R rating for a brief spurt of bad language or for one or two quick sequences with violent or sexual content that can be bypassed using the fast-forward button on the remote control. Likewise, a film bearing the milder PG or PG-13 rating may actually be loaded with obnoxious and offensive material. As with music, an excellent resource for detailed information about a film's content is *Plugged In*'s extensive Internet archive of film reviews (whether in current release or on DVD/Blu-ray) at www.pluggedin.com. *Plugged In* also provides extensive coverage of the content of TV programs.

Whatever you and your teenager watch or listen to, discuss the tone and content. Is this film, program, or song selling a viewpoint, and if so, what is it? If something struck you as offensive, why? Was there a positive message involved? What was it? Before your teen is finally living on her own, she's going to need to acquire enough discernment to find the wheat and avoid the chaff. Otherwise, while you may succeed in keeping every scrap of offensive material away from her eyes and ears during her high school years, she's eventually going to be exposed to at least some of it later on—but without your preparation or guidance.

How much "screen time" is reasonable for my teenager every day?

There is no hard and fast rule or magic number for this. However, many authorities (for example, the American Academy of Pediatrics) have weighed in with recommendations that children and adolescents be limited to two hours per day (or less) of TV, video games, or recreational computer activities. (This obviously does not include time spent doing homework on the computer.) Without outside limits, some children and adolescents will spend most of their waking hours in these physically passive (and frequently mind-numbing) pursuits.

How much privacy on the computer should I allow my teenager?

In a word, *none*. You reserve the right to know *everything* that enters and leaves your teenager's computer. Seriously consider implementing a house rule that online activity occurs only out in the open, where anyone can see what's on-screen, and not in a bedroom or behind closed doors. If you hear the objection, "But this is private stuff between me and my friends," it's time for a crucial reality check: By definition, anything posted online is no longer private. Even if only one or two people are meant to read it, they can easily pass it along to hundreds of others.

Your efforts to keep your teen out of harm's way on the Internet may meet with considerable resistance. Don't be surprised if his reaction to your expectations and limits implies that you're out of touch, a snoop, or worse. Listen to his concerns, but make sure he understands what's at stake and don't compromise his safety. If he doesn't like your rules, remind him that all of these technologies are optional and that using them is a privilege, not a right. Hopefully you won't need to resort to an ultimatum, but don't forget that until he's grown and gone, you're responsible for his safety, you're the parent, and you're in charge.

What limits should I suggest?

If you are concerned about the traffic coming and going into your teen's computer, you may want to install monitoring software that silently relays to you the content of every incoming and outgoing communication. (This is not the same as filtering software that can limit access to inappropriate material.) If you decide to install monitoring software in your adolescent's computer, be open about it and make clear that any attempt to inactivate it will lead to immediate loss of computer privileges. If your teenager knows that his computer is being monitored, he's likely to be more careful about what he says and where he goes online—and that's the whole point.

Should I allow my teen to post pictures on social networks?

If you allow your adolescent to establish a profile on a networking site such as Facebook or Twitter, you must be allowed access to it—and you should visit it often. (She should set the profile so that it can be accessed only by people she knows and to whom she has given permission to view it.)

One of many concerns related to teens spending hours engrossed in social networking sites, text messaging, and other forms of electronic interaction is that these are not face-to-face (or at least voice-to-voice) conversations. The nuances of inflection and facial expression—important elements of building relationships—are absent online, as are their restraining effects on inflammatory comments.

A twist on the oft-repeated ad slogan for Las Vegas should serve as a note of caution about the Internet: "What happens in cyberspace stays in cyberspace . . . indefinitely." Children and teenagers have unwisely posted provocative images of themselves and their friends, sensitive information about themselves and their families, and thoughts about their lives that would be more appropriately written in a journal that is locked in a desk drawer. Instead, this material can be read and passed around the world within seconds, *and it can't be taken back.* Some teens and college students have learned—to their chagrin—that teachers, employers, and even law-enforcement personnel have accessed embarrassing material, sometimes with very unpleasant results.

You might remind your teen never to allow anyone to photograph her partially or fully unclothed.

If your child or teenager would be uncomfortable having you, her pastor, teacher, employer, or future spouse see what she intends to send from her computer into cyberspace, *it shouldn't be sent.*

Your teenager needs to understand the importance of telling you if she receives any hostile or inappropriate content, including requests for personal information or a meeting. Any attempt to solicit a child to meet for sexual activity, or sending a child unsolicited obscene material online, is a criminal act that should be reported to law enforcement. For more information, check the CyberTipline at the website operated by the National Center for Missing and Exploited Children (www.missingkids.com).

What kind of rules should I set regarding cell phone use?

First of all, keep in mind that most cellular devices are much more than phones. They are powerful little computers that can send and receive all kinds of material, access the Internet, take photos and videos, play games, and so on. Unlike a desktop computer sitting in your home, this one is on the move, and tracking what comes in and goes out of it can be challenging.

Assuming that your teenager has earned the privilege of carrying a cell phone—remember, this is a *privilege*, not a right—you need to have one or more conversations during which you discuss the following:

- *How many calls and text messages can be made each month.* A 2009 Pew Research Center study found that half of teens surveyed sent more than fifty text messages per day, and one in three sent more than one hundred per day.[9] Does your cell plan allow for unlimited text messaging, or will you get a hefty bill when your teen dispatches thousands of texts each month?
- *Who can be called, how often, and when.* Are there charges for long distance or more than a certain number of calls per month? Assuming you don't want your teen calling or texting friends at all hours of the night (and you don't), there should be a reasonable "bedtime" for the phone.
- *Content of calls and messages.* As with social networking (which can also be done on mobile devices), texts with abusive or sexual content ("sexting") should be neither sent nor received by your adolescent's phone. Far too many kids have sent provocative photos of themselves or someone else to another person, only to find out that these images then spread like wildfire—often with disastrous results.

- *Talking or texting on the cell phone while driving.* Don't even think about it.
- *Behavior in front of someone else's phone camera.* All too often, kids who are goofing around, and perhaps pushing the crudity envelope, show up in someone's photos or videos, which are then posted on social networking sites or YouTube. The fallout can be embarrassing, or worse.
- *Monitoring will happen.* Just as with the computer, privacy isn't part of the deal. At the very least, you should check your monthly cell phone bill to see who your teen has called, and who has called her. For certain phones, monitoring software is available that will allow you to track incoming and outgoing phone calls, text messages, photos and videos taken, and websites accessed. By all means, look into this, and if you can find an appropriate program, install it on your teenager's phone. Let her know that you are doing this, and why. At this point in her life, you have the right and responsibility to ensure her safety and influence her decision making.
- *If your teen loses his phone, he pays for the replacement.*
- *The phone is subject to confiscation if misused.*

What about video games?

Electronic games (whether played on a home computer, smart phone, tablet device, or dedicated game system) are enormously popular with all age-groups and can consume vast amounts of time and money. Regardless of which platform(s) your teenager has available, you need to set specific limits on the time spent playing games—for *everyone* in your home. Kids aren't the only ones who can become hooked on electronic games. Adults can also spend hundreds of hours playing solitaire or become hopelessly entrenched in complex virtual worlds where they interact with thousands of other players on the Internet. (Believe it or not, marriages have been threatened, or even broken apart, when one partner became so immersed in an online game that she neglected basic responsibilities at home.)

Even if you have a good grip on the time factor, be careful about the content of games you or your kids buy, borrow, download, or rent. Though many are good, clean fun, some consist of non-stop fighting, and a few contain harsh language, vivid images of carnage and sex, or overtly antisocial themes. Sometimes these show up at advanced or deeper levels of the game, so once again you need to read up on the current electronic fare. As with music, movies, and TV programs, Focus on the Family's *Plugged In* website (www.pluggedin.com) contains detailed and insightful reviews of current electronic games on all platforms.

What do I need to know about pornography?

Pornography is a dangerous influence, one that encompasses a variety of media, including books, magazines, and videos. A few decades ago, someone who wanted to see a "skin flick" had to travel across town and sneak into a seedy theater where no one would recognize him. Since then, an explosion of new technologies has given pornography access to nearly every home. Most cable services offer not only unedited feature films and sexually explicit original programming on premium channels, but also a number of subscription and pay-per-view channels whose programming consists entirely of sexual material. Most major hotel chains offer pay-per-view movies in every room—including a selection of explicit "adult" films. The Internet has become a lawless frontier in which an adolescent—or an adult—is just a couple of mouse clicks away from a world of extraordinarily harsh and perverse material.

While some—especially those who advocate unrestricted access to anything by anyone—might characterize pornography as harmless (if mindless) entertainment, this material in fact has significant effects on attitudes and behavior. The blessings of sex—intimacy, bonding, sensitivity, commitment, sense of relationship, and reproduction—are not merely absent from pornography; they are routinely trampled by its unbridled promiscuity, shallowness, excesses (including violence), and utter stupidity. This might be dismissed as mere bad taste and lack of imagination were it not for a host of destructive effects, especially among the young.

Because pornography is so readily accessible in our culture, the sad reality is that you will need to talk about it with your child before and during adolescence, just as you will need to have an ongoing dialogue about other matters relating to sexuality. If you're having this conversation for the first time with a high school student, keep in mind that *he has probably already taken at least a cursory look at pornographic material*, especially if he has spent any amount of time on the Internet—even if you are fastidious about what you allow into your home. Many parents find out about this intrusion accidentally, perhaps stumbling onto some sexually provocative or even hard-core material while cleaning out a teen's closet, turning his mattress, or checking the history and cookie files on his computer, which can tell you the websites he has been visiting. Whether your conversation is planned or provoked by a discovery that he's been looking at unsavory material, keep the following principles in mind.

What if I find out that my teenager has been looking at pornography?

Remember and acknowledge that he is curious about sexuality—just as you were—and that this is normal. If he has made a commitment to keep his mind and body unpolluted, great—but he's still curious. However, he needs to understand that pornography is the worst source of information about this subject, that it exploits women, that it can be both addictive and progressive, and that it is very offensive.

Avoid extremes. If you shrug off involvement with pornography as harmless "boys will be boys" entertainment, you're missing both the importance of the issue and the opportunity to instill some key values. If you preach a forty-five-minute sermon, especially one that includes a lot of exclamations of shock and shame, you'll drive him into secrecy rather than inspire accountability.

The best approach is to be calm, straightforward, and matter-of-fact, but very clear about your principles. Indeed, the tone of your conversation can have a serious impact on your ability to broach some critical topics: If he has been looking at pornography, how long and how often has it occurred? Is he a habitual user? Has he been trying to break free of it? You won't find out if you approach this topic with verbal guns blazing.

Someone struggling with pornography will need more than a single discussion to overcome this compulsion. Entrenched behavior that has strong reinforcement rarely disappears easily. Confronting the problem, becoming educated about it, accepting responsibility for one's actions, taking practical steps to limit exposure to provocative material, and maintaining accountability with others who are willing to exercise tough love are all part of the process. Some resources you might consider include:

- *Wired for Intimacy: How Pornography Hijacks the Male Brain* by William Struthers (IVP Books, 2010).
- *Help! Someone I Know Has a Problem with Porn* by Jim Vigorito (Focus on the Family, 2006).
- Focus on the Family's TroubledWith.com website includes the section "Pornography and Cybersex," offering practical information and useful links.
- A number of topics related to sexuality, including pornography, sexual addiction, and raising children with healthy attitudes toward sexuality, are discussed at another Focus on the Family site, www.pureintimacy.org.

By the way, there are many households in which an adolescent isn't the only person struggling with pornography. If Dad (or perhaps an older sibling) has been dealing with this issue, everyone needs to be on the same page. A double standard on this or any other behavioral question is unacceptable. In addition, depending on the status of family communications, some candid and transparent conversation could establish a bond and an environment of accountability that would go a long way toward a permanent household ban on this noxious product.

If you learn that your teenager has been delving into more malignant pornographic realms such as homosexuality, violence, or material involving children, you will need to go a step further and get him involved in counseling with a qualified individual who shares your basic views on sexuality.

CHAPTER 4

A PARENT'S GUIDE TO TEEN SEXUALITY

Do not stir up or awaken love
until the appropriate time.

SONG OF SONGS 2:7, HCSB

THIS CHAPTER WILL focus repeatedly on an important principle: It is appropriate, wise, and potentially lifesaving to teach your kids to wait until marriage to become sexually active.

God designed sex to bring new life into existence, to generate a powerful bond between a husband and wife, and to be intensely pleasurable. It is a wonderful, extraordinary, and powerful gift that deserves to be treated with great and abiding respect. In the context of a permanent and public commitment, it can be savored, explored, and nurtured without guilt or fear of serious consequences. But at the wrong time with the wrong person, sex can bring disappointment and disease, as well as derail life plans and purposes.

Your adolescent, who is curious about and highly interested in sex, needs a clearheaded understanding of its benefits and risks in order to make a serious commitment to establish, maintain, or restore sexual integrity. Maintaining such a commitment won't always be easy.

Why is it so challenging to preserve the gift of sex for marriage?

Inner drives. Every adolescent has sexual interests and feelings. No one passes through the teen years devoid of sexual urges. Just like anyone else, teens deeply need love and affirmation. As a result, they can become emotionally and sexually attracted to others around them and drawn toward physical intimacy. But they also enter adolescence with a sense of modesty that tends to inhibit sexual exploration.

These realities were clearly recognized just a few generations ago, when modesty was encouraged and more formal boundaries were set between unmarried members of the opposite sex. Today, many would call such efforts stuffy, inhibited, and puritanical. But our ancestors were in many ways more "streetwise" about adolescent sexuality and made it somewhat easier for their sons and daughters to resist sexual pressure. Our culture, on the other hand, practically drowns kids in temptation.

Provocative images and messages. Sex sells everything, from beer to burgers, and from cars to chewing gum. Images that tantalize young men in particular are everywhere—department-store lingerie ads, the *Sports Illustrated* swimsuit edition, and countless magazine covers in the supermarket checkout line. These images also speak powerfully to young women: *This is what guys want*.

Seductive messages. During the late 1960s, a cultural upheaval, sometimes called the sexual revolution, assaulted traditional expectations for sexual behavior. Virtually all popular media (movies, TV, DVDs, music) as well as educational, health care, and governmental organizations were affected by this moral free fall. As a result, by the time your child arrives at puberty, she will have heard the following destructive messages many, many times and in a variety of ways:

- Sex is okay any way and with anyone (even someone you just met a few minutes ago), as long as there is mutual consent, no one gets pregnant (unless she wants to), and no one gets hurt.
- Sex is usual and customary if you are attracted to someone.
- Sex unrelated to marriage is normal, natural, expected, and inevitable, so carry a condom and know how to use it correctly.
- If you are postponing sex until marriage, you must be incredibly unattractive, socially inept, or fanatically committed to some type of prudish or fundamentalist religion.

Hearing "anything goes" and "everyone's doing it" over and over can be difficult for teenagers to ignore. Under the assault of these messages, even those who are committed to preserving sex for marriage may begin to feel as if they are completely out of step and needlessly missing out on one of life's greatest pleasures.

Lack of supervision. Because of fragmented families, complex parental work schedules, easier access to transportation, and (at times) carelessness among adults who should know better, adolescents today are more likely to find opportunities to be alone together for long stretches of time. In such circumstances, even teens who have made a commitment to wait for sex until their wedding night can find it much more difficult to keep their promises to God, to themselves, and to their future spouse.

An overbearing, overprotective atmosphere at home. Adolescents who are smothered in a controlled, micromanaged, suspicious environment are strong candidates for rebellion once the opportunity arises. When restraints are tightly enforced in an atmosphere of ongoing mistrust, kids may be tempted to become sexually involved simply to "get it over with," to see what all the fuss is about, and to assert their independence. Ironically, a big (and dangerous) rebellion may represent an effort to break loose from an overabundance of trivial constraints.

Peer pressure. This ever-present influence comes in three powerful forms:

- *A general sense that "everyone is doing it except me."* Movies, TV, videos, and popular music nurture this idea. Conversations with friends or even offhanded comments overheard between strangers may bring the idea closer to home. If your school district's health-education curriculum emphasizes contraception and condom use, but barely mentions abstinence, it will foster the notion that "everyone is having sex." The weight of this "evidence" may lead a young person to conclude, "These professionals know more about this than I do. I must be the only seventeen-year-old in town who hasn't had sex."
- *Apparent widespread acceptance of casual, recreational, or "disposable" sexual contact.* For example, many of today's adolescents do not consider oral sex to be sex—a fanciful notion that can have disastrous consequences—or they consider it to be less intimate or less meaningful than intercourse. While at parties, many adolescents and college students have experienced "hooking up"—a spontaneous physical (usually sexual) encounter disconnected from any ongoing relationship. The term "friends with benefits" (and other far more crude variations) is commonly used for individuals who engage in sexual activity without any expectation from the relationship, romantic or otherwise.

All of these reflect a naive, but all too common, notion that sex can be experienced not only without physical consequences but also without any relationship or emotional fallout.

• *Direct pressure from another person who wants a sexual experience, or an invitation from a willing potential partner.* Come-ons, smooth talk, whining, haggling, and outright coercion by males who want sex are timeworn negative behaviors. A young woman's resistance may be lowered by a need for closeness and acceptance, and the mistaken belief that physical intimacy will secure a man's love. In recent years, this turnabout has become common: A young man is informed by his girlfriend (or a new acquaintance) that she wants to have sex with him. Personal convictions that sex is intended for marriage will be put to the ultimate test in a situation like this, especially if some physical contact is already under way. A young man's moral code and all the admonitions he has heard may suddenly seem terribly abstract, while the intense pleasure that is his for the taking is very real. Which will prevail?

Lack of reasons (or desire) to wait. Some adolescents are determined to have sex, regardless of the risks. Others are unshakably committed to the goal that their first and only sex partner will be their spouse. In between these opposite poles live a large number of teenagers who keep an informal mental tally of reasons for and against premarital sex. Inner longings and external pressure pull them toward it, while standards taught at home and church, medical warnings, and commonsense restraints put on the brakes.

For many teenagers (even those who intend to abstain until marriage), decisions about sex tend to be made based on the drift of this internal "vote count." When the moment of truth arrives, the tally may be close—or a landslide in the wrong direction. It may even result in an approach—what some call serial monogamy—that attempts to reconcile what are in fact incompatible positions: "I'll be careful with my health and emotions by having sex with only one person at any given time." Adolescents with a shaky or negative self-concept may be particularly vulnerable to sexual involvement if they think it might win approval from someone whom they perceive to be attractive or popular.

How can I make a case for abstinence?

Without being overbearing or obsessive, make an effort to have ongoing dialogues with your teenager about the many compelling reasons to postpone sex until the wedding night. (It goes without saying that you should be talking to your teenager about many things besides areas of concern and danger. If your communication is smooth in other, less-volatile areas, it will likely flow more easily with a sensitive topic such as sexuality.) The following list of reasons to wait may help you formulate and express your thoughts during these important conversations.

Reason to wait #1: The moral high ground. Despite the rising tide of sexual anarchy in our society, a great many people still believe the words *right* and *wrong* apply to sexual behavior. Even someone with a casual exposure to traditional Judeo-Christian values should pick up an important message: God, who designed us as sexual beings, cares a lot about when we have sex and with whom. Sex outside of marriage can be dangerous to one's physical, emotional, and spiritual health. Even for those who do not follow specific religious precepts, basic decency and concern for the well-being of others should curtail the vast majority of sexual adventures, which often are loaded with selfish agendas.

Unfortunately, some teens who have had ongoing church experiences and explicit teaching about sexual morality may still become involved in premarital sex, which does nothing for their spiritual growth. Intimacy with God on Sunday morning (or any other day) will be seriously impaired when physical intimacy the night before has clearly violated the boundaries set forth in Scripture.

Reason to wait #2: Sex is how babies get started. Each year, hundreds of thousands of American teenagers become pregnant, and approximately three in ten of these pregnancies end in abortion. The vast majority of these pregnancies are unplanned, and a sizable percentage begin even though a contraceptive is used.

These statistics do not begin to communicate the profound effects of a pregnancy on a young woman's life. Whatever the circumstances of the sexual encounter that began it, a pregnancy cannot be ignored, and whatever is done about it will have a permanent impact on the young mother's life. Once she becomes pregnant, she will never be the same. Only two outcomes are possible: The baby will be born, or the baby will die before birth, whether through deliberate abortion or spontaneous miscarriage. Neither of these events is easy to deal with. There's no quick fix where human life is concerned, no way to start over as if nothing happened.

An abortion is not a completely risk-free procedure. Damage to the uterus that could jeopardize future pregnancies (or even require major surgical repair), infection, bleeding, future infertility, and even more serious events (including death) are possible complications, though rare. Furthermore, even if an abortion is performed without any apparent hitch, a different type of pain may develop months or years later. Because most young women in this situation want so desperately for the crisis to go away, many will undergo an abortion even though they are knowingly violating their own moral standards. Many come to realize later in life that a human being—a son or a daughter, not a shapeless wad of tissue—was destroyed through abortion.

As with many issues related to crisis pregnancies, a pregnancy resource center (which in your community may be called a crisis pregnancy center, pregnancy care center, or women's resource center) may offer support for women who are dealing with the emotional aftermath of an abortion. You can also obtain help from organizations such as Care Net (www.care-net.org) or Option Line (www.optionline.org).

If an unmarried teenager bears and brings up her child, her life (and probably the lives of other family members) will be affected for years to come. She must deal with the many challenges that all new mothers face, but nearly always with some additional difficulties. Her educational plans are likely to be postponed or significantly rearranged. (Fewer than four out of ten teenage girls eighteen and under who bear a child will earn a high school diploma.)[10] Unless she has considerable help and support, a teenage mother will risk difficulties with parenting, difficulty in a future marriage relationship, and more unplanned pregnancies.

If a young mother places her child for adoption—an act of considerable courage—she will help bring about what is often a relatively positive combination of outcomes. Her baby will be reared by people who are usually better prepared to provide the time, attention, and resources. She in turn can move on with her education and social life. But even this solution will not exempt her from pain. She will never forget her baby, and she may experience a sense of loss, sometimes profound, for the rest of her life.

Reason to wait #3: Sexually transmitted infections (STIs). Fifty years ago, the typical high school health-education class discussed two types of sexually transmitted infections: *syphilis* and *gonorrhea*. They were described as potentially hazardous infections, but nothing a little penicillin couldn't handle. But the shift in sexual mores that took root during the late 1960s has resulted in an ongoing STI epidemic populated with exotic, dangerous, and often incurable infections.

More than twenty significant diseases can be transmitted skin to skin or by exchange of bodily fluids during sexual activity. Some are fatal, a few are relatively harmless, and many have long-term physical and emotional consequences. A few can be successfully treated with antibiotics—but without creating long-term immunity. As a result, infections such as gonorrhea and chlamydia can be acquired repeatedly by the same individual.

Reason to wait #4: The risk of infertility. Millions of couples have difficulty conceiving, and more than a million couples seek treatment for infertility each year in the United States. Statistics cannot begin to reflect the intense distress this problem creates in a couple's life. Dealing with infertility can be complicated, time-consuming, stressful, and expensive—whereas the process of starting a pregnancy is designed to be pleasurable and free. Unfortunately, a significant number (but not all) of these infertility problems arise as a consequence of sexually transmitted infections and thus could have been avoided if both husband and wife had postponed sex until marriage.

Reason to wait #5: To preserve the value of sex. Advocating that sex be kept within the boundaries of marriage is not based on notions that intercourse is "dirty" or "unholy," but on a true appreciation for sex as God's fine art. If the original *Mona Lisa* were entrusted to you for a month, you wouldn't leave it in your backyard, use it as a TV tray, or line a birdcage with it. Similarly, sex deserves more respect than our culture gives it.

Reason to wait #6: To prevent distorted relationships. Adding sex to a nonmarital relationship, especially when teens are involved, is like throwing a half-ton boulder into a rowboat. The center of gravity shifts drastically, forward motion becomes difficult, and the boat may eventually sink. Sex never enhances a teenage romance, but almost always overwhelms and stifles it. Arguments, secrecy, stress, and guilt usually replace laughter, discovery, and meaningful conversation.

Indeed, sex has a way of wrecking good relationships and keeping bad ones going long after they should have ended. After a sexual relationship has broken off, there is likely to be a sense of loss (sometimes severe), regret, and awkwardness whenever the other person is encountered. Condoms can't prevent a broken heart, and antibiotics can't cure one.

Reason to wait #7: To avoid devaluing one's sexuality and identity. An important warning for teenage girls: In the sexual revolution, women have been—and still are—the big losers. When an unwanted pregnancy occurs, the woman virtually always pays a far bigger price than her partner. Also, with the exception of syphilis and AIDS, many sexually transmitted infections have more serious consequences in women.

When young women accept the philosophy of "sex as recreation," they give away a number of sexual encounters and ultimately receive nothing in return—no ongoing relationship, no security, no commitments, no love, and possibly no children in the future (if they acquire a pelvic infection from a partner).

But there is another critical arena in which far too many women have reaped a bitter harvest from seeds sown during the sexual revolution: the devaluation of their sexuality and their very identity. For a woman, the ability to enjoy an uninhibited and healthy sexual response requires that her sexual experiences begin in a setting of complete trust, respect, and love. But this nurturing context is very uncommon when sexual activity first occurs in a nonmarital relationship, even if she is feeling desperately "in love" with her partner. Instead, all too often, adolescent sex occurs in an immature, predatory, or even abusive relationship.

The consequences from such encounters can be devastating. One be a strong sense of having been used, violated, and devalued. Instead of learning from experience and resolving not to be burned again, a sexually experienced adolescent—especially one for whom sex has not been entirely voluntary—is likely to think, *What does it matter now? I might as well just go ahead the next time.* Without specific counseling to counteract this mentality, resistance to continuing sexual activity may be seriously weakened. (This devaluation of both sexuality and self, while generally more common and profound in girls, certainly occurs in boys as well. Girls and boys alike can be emotionally devastated by the breakup of a relationship that involves sexual intimacy.)

Another likely consequence of early nonmarital sexual experiences is that a young woman's sense of self-worth may become linked to her sexual usefulness to others. Ironically, even though she may look and act sexually sophisticated, her ability to *respond* sexually is almost certain to be compromised—an issue that may come home to roost if and when she marries. Rather than being enjoyed in an uncomplicated way, sex is more likely to be experienced as a complex and often contradictory mixture of functions: as currency and power in a relationship or as a source of anxiety over a partner's approval.

What issues increase the risk of my child engaging in premarital sex?

You may not be able to prevent your teen from having sex, but you can reduce the likelihood by being aware of the specific risk factors for teen sex:

Alcohol and drug use. Aside from reflecting problem attitudes (rebellion, poor self-concept, a mistaken sense of invulnerability) that make sex more likely, intoxication also clouds judgment and weakens resistance to sexual overtures.

A steady boyfriend or girlfriend. Strong attachments and feelings of exclusivity invite nature to take its course, especially when physical expressions of affection begin early in the relationship. *This is a particular risk in a situation where the boy is more than two or three years older than the girl.* Ideally, a take-it-slow approach to relationships can be encouraged and set in motion through conversations both before and during the adolescent years. If a teen romance appears to be getting hot and heavy and a lot of physical contact is already displayed, you will have a more delicate task. You will need to speak diplomatically but candidly with both teenagers about the physical process they are setting in motion. If you're too easygoing about it, you will do little to discourage further progress down the road toward intimacy. On the other hand, if you come down too hard, you may drive the young lovers closer together, emotionally and physically. Forbidding further contact (which is much easier said than done) should be reserved for situations in which it is clear that the relationship is damaging, dangerous, or abusive.

Little parental monitoring. Teenagers aren't likely to remove their clothing and get horizontal if parents are in the next room. Leaving a young man and woman alone for hours at a time, or not requiring accountability, is a setup for sex.

A parental belief that adolescent sex is appropriate. If you think nonmarital sex is okay, your son or daughter will, too, and will act on that belief.

A parental belief that adolescent sex is inevitable. Many parents who disapprove of teen sex have also concluded that it is as certain as death and taxes. Thus their approach to the subject can sound like double-talk: "Don't do it, but in case you do, be sure to use a condom." A few take their daughter to a doctor or a family-planning clinic to obtain birth control pills—*even if she has not become sexually active.* In sexual matters, invoking the venerable motto "Be prepared" communicates not only precaution, but also expectation: *I know you're going to do it.* Teens will get that message loud and clear and are likely to act accordingly.

Low grade point average/low attachment to school. Though academic performance is affected by a variety of factors, a basic desire to do well in school reflects (among other things) a more hopeful outlook on the future and a willingness to put off immediate gratification for long-term goals. Teen sex, on the contrary, is a here-and-now event, usually reflecting ignorance of or little regard for consequences. This doesn't mean, of course, that every scholar is a bulwark of morality or that all who are not academically oriented are destined to be promiscuous. What ultimately matters is a person's commitment to basic values such as responsibility, respect for self and others, and concern about the effect of today's decisions on the future.

A history of physical or sexual abuse. Abusive acts against children and teens violate their bodies, minds, and hearts. Sexual abuse creates a grossly distorted view of sexual behavior, destroys boundaries, and drives a deep sense of worthlessness into the teenager's emotions. Whether the abuse occurred in the distant or recent past, teens who have been abused need ongoing support, counseling, and prayer to help them develop healthy attitudes about sex and about themselves.

Frequent family relocations. Moving is generally stressful for both parents and teens (especially if the kids resent the decision).

This can erode parental authority and distract parents from involvement with their children. Bonds to social supports such as church groups that help prevent sexual activity are severed by multiple moves. Loneliness and loss of friendships may lead some teenagers to use sexual activity as a means to gain social acceptance. These issues should be considered by parents who are thinking about a possible relocation.

Only one parent in the household. Parenting was meant to be a team effort, and some risks will naturally increase when one parent is left to do all the protecting and monitoring alone. Some studies indicate that teens living with a single parent are more likely to become sexually active than those living with both parents. Work and household demands can prevent single parents from being as involved and attentive as they need and want to be. And the divorce or desertion that sometimes leads to a one-parent home can make teens uncertain about the value of marriage as the setting for sexual activity.

This increased risk does not mean that adolescent sex is inevitable in single-parent families. But it does place an additional responsibility on single parents to send their teenagers clear and consistent messages about sexuality. And it is one more reason for single parents to enlist as much support as they can.

What can I do to reduce my teen's likelihood of becoming sexually active?

Although the issues mentioned previously can set the stage for teen sex, there are steps you can take to reduce the likelihood of your child's involvement.

Encourage supervised, structured, non-pressuring group activities with the opposite sex, as opposed to single dating situations, especially for teens in middle school and early high school. The object should be to learn how to talk and have fun without romantic expectations or sexual pressure.

Be aware of factors that lower the risk for teen sex, including:

- religious commitment
- friends who have a similar commitment to abstinence
- presence of both parents in the home, especially the biological father
- involvement in extracurricular interests either in or outside of school
- parental and community values that support and clearly promote sexual abstinence until marriage

Your influence on your teen's choices related to sexual activity cannot be overestimated. Here are some specific ways you can encourage your teen to abstain from premarital sexual activity.

Be a role model for the kinds of relationships you want your kids to develop with members of the opposite sex. Parents should make every effort to keep their marriage intact and to nourish, enrich, and celebrate it, demonstrating respect and affection for each other on an ongoing basis. This gives teens a sense of security and a strong attachment to parental values.

Fathers have a particularly important role to play. A boy who sees his father treat his mother with physical and verbal courtesies (which may range from fine points such as opening doors for her to broader strokes such as regularly seeking her opinions and advice, and listening to and praising her) and is taught to do likewise will be more likely to carry this behavior and attitude into his own relationships with women. Girls who are consistently affirmed, cherished, and treated respectfully by their fathers aren't as likely to begin a desperate search for male affection that could lead to sexual involvement. Furthermore, they will expect appropriate behavior from the other men in their lives.

Single parents who are bringing up teenagers must repeatedly affirm them and create as stable a home life as possible. Values concerning nonmarital sex should be practiced as well as preached. A sexually active single parent or one who has a live-in partner is proclaiming in no uncertain terms that this activity is all right for teenagers as well.

Do your best to give your teenager a strong, positive sense of identity. Teenagers who feel incomplete, inadequate, and unappreciated are more likely to seek comfort in a sexual relationship. But those with a life rich in relationships, family traditions, activities, interests, and—most of all—consistent love and affirmation are less likely to embark on a desperate search for fulfillment that could lead to unwise sexual decisions. Those who see their future as promising are more likely to protect themselves from physical or emotional damage arising from sexual activity. Those who have a healthy, productive faith in God are more likely to have deeply rooted reasons to respect and preserve the gift of sex and to respect rather than exploit others.

Create a special occasion to talk about abstaining from sex until marriage. Early in your child's adolescence, plan a special evening (or a weekend away from home) during which the importance of preserving sex for marriage is the central focus. This time, shared by the teen and both parents, could culminate in the presentation of a special token—a necklace, ring, or key, for example—that symbolizes commitment to an abstinent lifestyle. It can be very meaningful if this item is carried or worn by your adolescent for years and then presented to her marriage partner on their wedding night.

If your adolescent has already had sexual experiences, make it clear that it is never too late to make a commitment to reserve sex for marriage. This important concept is called "secondary virginity" and should be strongly encouraged among teens who have been sexually active. Some churches and parachurch organizations have formal programs organized specifically to promote the decision to remain sexually abstinent until marriage.

How can I communicate with my teen about sex?

The best time to build a solid foundation for healthy sexuality is before puberty. But even if you've never discussed the subject directly, you still send all kinds of signals about your attitudes over the course of time.

Continue sending healthy messages about sexuality throughout your son's or daughter's adolescent years. Your adolescent needs to know you are comfortable with the subject. If you seem embarrassed, flustered, ashamed, or unapproachable whenever the topic comes up, your teenager will look elsewhere for input.

Don't hesitate to broach the subject yourself. Teens are reluctant to bring up sexual subjects with their parents, and your chances of having one or more conversations may be nil unless you take the initiative. Remember that the facts of sexuality are morally neutral. Anyone (even you) can teach them, but you have the opportunity to put the proper perspective on the subject.

Be careful how you talk about someone else's sexual issues. News of a crisis pregnancy in another family can provide a powerful teachable moment, for good or ill. If you give a clear signal that the nonmarital sex was wrong but respond with compassion (and prayer) for the people involved, you make it clear that you can be approached if anyone at home has a problem. But if your response sounds something like "Don't you ever do something as stupid/shameful/evil as this," you could block potentially vital

communication in the future. Pregnancy resource centers routinely find that many of their most difficult clients are the daughters of good, moral, upright, churchgoing parents. "I can't tell
Mom and Dad—it'll kill them (or they'll kill me)" is a common
refrain as these girls head for an abortion clinic.

**Talk about healthy and unhealthy relationships, and train
your adolescent to avoid situations that increase the likelihood of a sexual incident.** Group activities such as a church pic-
nic or youth-group outing are generally healthier than dances or
other situations in which pairing up is necessary.

Talk to your teen about the qualities that ultimately matter in
a relationship with a person of the opposite sex. Shared values
(especially spiritual orientation), mutual respect, easy conversation, and enjoyment of everyday activities count far more heavily
in the long run than good looks, money, popularity, or intense
romantic attraction. Indeed, the best romances and marriages
often come from relaxed friendships that progress gradually, with
lots of conversations about everything under the sun. Accordingly,
dating activities should be seen as experiences that are pleasant,
enriching, and relaxing, not times of perpetual emotion.

Talk to your teen about unhealthy relationships, and have the
courage to speak honestly if you see one developing in one or more
of the following ways:

- Relationships that ride a roller coaster of emotions—where
  two people are madly in love one day, fight like cats and
  dogs the next, and then cry and make up over and over—
  distract and drain a couple's time and energy and wear out
  everyone else around them. They are also a setup for sexual
  involvement, as the passionate fight often concludes with
  equally passionate reconciliation (what many couples refer

to as "makeup sex"). This type of turbulent relationship is likely to turn into an even stormier marriage.

- Relationships in which one person is intensely clingy and smothering. For example, the woeful refrain, "I'd kill myself if you ever left me" puts inappropriate and unhealthy pressure on the other person.
- Relationships that have ongoing verbal disrespect in one or both directions are doomed.
- Relationships in which physical abuse occurs must be terminated immediately.

Talk to your adolescent about physical demonstrations of affection. This is a natural desire when two people like each other, but how much (and how far) is okay? What about handling the desire—or some pressure—to push physical boundaries? You can lay down rules and regulations, but your adolescent needs a rationale for making good decisions without you. Here are some ideas that may help your teenager.

Establish your expectations and ground rules about dating in advance—well before your teenager asks if she can go out with someone. Each family will have to set its own standards, but extremes are best avoided. Rigid parental control through high school and beyond (including selecting a limited number of "acceptable" candidates for courtship) stifles growth and independence and virtually guarantees rebellion. But a lax, anything-goes approach without parental guidelines is like handing the car keys to someone who has had no driver's training.

Think seriously about adopting a stepwise approach, especially for your adolescent's first socializing experiences with the opposite sex. Many parents have a policy that if someone wants to spend time with their son or daughter under age eighteen, the first step is spending an evening at home with the family or joining in a family activity such as dinner and a movie or a ball game. This gives everyone a chance to get acquainted and broadcasts an important message: *The one you want to spend time with is deeply cherished by a family to whom you are accountable. We are happy to welcome you aboard, but nothing less than respectful and honorable behavior will do.* Your expectation should be to make friends with the person, not to carry out a third-degree interrogation. In fact, you may develop a friendship that lasts long after your son or daughter has become interested in someone else. If anyone refuses or is extremely reluctant to spend time with the family in this way, however, consider it a red flag—and put further socializing with this person on hold.

If the first step goes well, group dating can be a good way to continue this process, assuming the other people involved are trustworthy. Many parents give the green light to single dating at age sixteen if there is ongoing evidence of maturity and responsibility and if the relationship appears basically healthy. Whenever this activity begins, you have the right and responsibility to know specifics every time, including the intended companion(s), the activity and its location, who's providing transportation, etc. Have a clear agreement about the expected time to arrive home. Whatever time you set, talk about the importance of your teenager letting you know if he is going to be home later than planned. Consistency and reliability about keeping you posted should be a bigger issue than abiding by an absolute time limit.

Though your son or daughter may complain outwardly about some of these ground rules, most teens will feel more secure when their parents are appropriately involved in the socializing/dating process. This should extend beyond setting limits to offering some encouragement as well, such as quietly providing a little extra cash to help enhance a special occasion. Even more important is making it abundantly clear that your teenager can call you anytime, day or night, from anywhere, if any help is needed—including a ride home from a date that has gone sour.

Should I talk with my teen about masturbation?

At some point during these years, you will need to deal with the subject of masturbation. It is extremely likely that masturbation leading to sexual climax will occur at some point, especially for a male. If he is racked with guilt about it and repeatedly vows never to let it happen again, he will probably expend a lot of energy feeling like a moral failure and worrying unnecessarily about his spiritual welfare. But when masturbation becomes a routine and frequent habit, especially when accompanied by vivid sexual fantasies or, worse, the viewing of pornography, it can be damaging to sexual and emotional health.

Your approach to this issue will need to be both tactful and realistic. *A bottom line worth stressing is that masturbation should not play a major role in your child's life, either as a source of relentless guilt or as a frequent and persistent habit that displaces healthy sexual relations in the future.* If it happens once in a while, it happens. But it should not be pursued as a form of recreation, especially while viewing sexually provocative materials, and it should never be allowed to occur with other people.

Who should deliver this message? In many families, everyone will feel more comfortable if mothers talk with daughters and fathers with sons. It may be more fruitful, however, if both parents participate in this and other discussions of sexuality. Such sensitive issues should always be discussed privately, of course, with only one child at a time.

What can I do if I discover my teenager is sexually active?

Many contemporary resources for parents of teenagers make the wrong assumption that premarital sex is inevitable and recommend that parents help their kids make "mature" sexual decisions—by which they mean wearing condoms and taking other contraceptive precautions. Some parents respond by bringing their teenage (or even preteen) daughters to a doctor or a family-planning clinic for various birth-control measures and insisting that their teen-agers not go out for the evening without a supply of condoms.

If facilitating adolescent sex is a bad idea, so is ignoring it. Equally unproductive is blowing up, finger wagging, lecturing, or name-calling. Teenage sexual activity is a significant family issue that deserves a loving and thoughtful response. The goal is to con-tain the damage and coach your adolescent toward more healthy and rational decisions. When discussing your teenager's sexual activity, keep the following guidelines in mind:

Think before you react. It is normal to feel upset and disap-pointed, and you will probably need a couple of days to process the information. Setting a time to talk about what has happened may be more appropriate than risking a more volatile, spur-of-the-moment confrontation. Ultimately, your emotions should fuel appropriate action rather than ignite angry outbursts.

Ask open-ended questions rather than judgmental ones. Listen to the whole story (or as much as you are given) before offer-ing your viewpoint. Eye rolling, crossed arms, finger drumming, and editorial comments will shut off communication in a hurry.

Put the emphasis on the big picture. You want your son or daughter to have a long life, good health, meaningful relation-ships, and freedom from unnecessary turmoil. Premarital sexual activity jeopardizes all of those goals.

Don't tear down your teenager's sense of worth with com-ments such as "I am so ashamed of you" or "How could you act like such a jerk/tramp/lowlife?" This kind of rejection and judgment is what drives a lot of teens to sexual activity.

Stress the importance of new beginnings. Many teens who have been sexually active are willing to commit to secondary virginity, postponing any further sexual relationships until marriage. Actively encourage such a decision. Otherwise the feeling that "it doesn't matter anymore" may lead to more bad decisions.

Get medical input. A doctor's evaluation should be on the agenda to check for STIs (and for girls, to obtain a Pap test or perhaps a pregnancy test). Choose your provider carefully. Your adolescent is less likely to choose abstinence if she has a doctor who feels that teens can't control their sexual urges and who therefore emphasizes methods of contraception.

Strongly consider counseling for your son or daughter (and yourself). A counselor whom you trust may be able to talk more candidly to your son or daughter about sexuality while promoting the decision to remain abstinent. Sexual activity may be a symptom of more basic problems that need ongoing work. Be prepared to invest your own time with the counselor to deal with the causes and effects of this problem within your family.

Be prepared to take action appropriate for the situation and the age of your adolescent. Sexual activity in the elementary or middle-school grades deserves a highly concerted effort from parents, physicians, counselors, and others (a trusted youth-group leader at church, for example) to deal with the behavior and with underlying issues. A sexually active twelve- or thirteen-year-old has experienced a serious breach of physical and emotional boundaries, and considerable work will be needed to repair the damage.

You may need to have one or more candid conversations with your adolescent's partner(s) and possibly with the parents of the other individual(s) as well. More often than not, this will lead to one or more relationships being terminated and implementation of much tighter supervision and accountability. Parental schedules may need to be rearranged. If the situation involves an adult having sexual contact with a young adolescent, legal action may be necessary. (At the very least, an adult's sexual activity with a minor must be reported as required by law. Any indications of coercion and abuse must also be reported.)

Sexual activity in high school is no less significant, but the response (including medical and counseling input) should represent more of a parent-directed collaboration between the adolescent and the teachers, counselors, and physicians involved in her life. This does not mean abandoning efforts to curtail sexual contact but using strategies that emphasize a mature assessment of consequences. Dating and other socializing patterns that may have increased the chances for intimacy should be reassessed and restructured.

What are the risks of oral sex?

Though oral sex—contact between one person's mouth or tongue and another person's genitals—isn't typically a topic of polite conversation, a surprising number of people don't perceive oral sex as sex. This view is often accompanied by a dangerous—and false—belief that oral sex isn't particularly risky. This belief is especially common among teenagers.

Some adolescent girls who practice oral sex consider themselves to be virgins or sexually abstinent. Health-care providers or counselors who attempt to obtain an accurate sexual history from teenagers must routinely ask not only "Are you sexually active?" but also "Are you giving or receiving oral sex?" It is not uncommon for a teenager or young adult to answer no to the first question and yes to the second. Even significant numbers of college students consider oral sex compatible with a sexually abstinent lifestyle. This idea is both emotionally and morally naive—and it may be medically misinformed, as well, if it assumes oral sex is risk-free. Though it is true that pregnancy will not result from oral sex, a number of sexually transmitted infections can be spread through oral-genital contact, including syphilis, gonorrhea, herpes simplex virus, HPV, chlamydia, and even HIV. The potential consequences can range from a sore throat (from gonorrhea) or hoarseness (from HPV) to serious systemic illness (syphilis), throat cancer (again, from HPV), and even death (HIV/AIDS).

How can I protect my daughter from date rape and other sexual assault?

Talk candidly to your daughter about the unpleasant topic of date rape and how best to avoid it. The odds are at least one in six that a woman will be coerced into unwanted sex at some point in her life. In four out of five cases, the rapist is someone the woman knows—a fellow student, a business acquaintance, a neighbor, or (all too often) a date.

For your part, aside from issuing specific recommendations and warnings, set some policies that will reduce the risk of a sexual catastrophe. First, veto any dating relationship between your adolescent daughter and someone who is more than two or three years older. The majority of teenage pregnancies involve relationships with men in their twenties or older. Object vigorously to her dating anyone who might have a position of authority or leverage over some part of her life, such as an employer, teacher, family friend, or business associate of yours. These situations are a setup for potential date rape.

Here are some rules and warnings you can talk over with your daughter:

- You are much better off dating someone you know fairly well rather than someone who is a casual or chance acquaintance. Be leery of someone you met through a social network or anywhere else online.

- In general, multi-couple or group activities are less risky (and more fun) than single dates.
- Single dates—especially the first time with someone— should take place in public places. An invitation to a play or a sporting event is by far preferable to "Come to my place to watch a movie." Be especially wary of the suggestion that it would be nice "to go someplace private to talk."
- Consider accepting a blind date only if the person carries a strong endorsement from someone you trust.
- Stay sober. Alcohol and drugs cloud judgment and put a person off guard and off balance.
- Never leave a restaurant, party, or other get-together with someone you just met.
- Trust your instincts. If you don't feel right about the way the date is progressing, bail out.
- Avoid situations in which you do not feel on equal footing with your companion. If you feel intimidated, awestruck, or indebted to your date in some way, your willingness to assert yourself may be weakened or delayed. Unhealthy situations include relationships with men more than two or three years older, an employer, a teacher, or someone to whom you or your family owes a debt.
- Beware of expensive gifts and lavish dates. Too many guys still carry the Neanderthal notion that picking up the tab for a nice evening entitles them to a sexual "thank you." If your date presents that message, don't hesitate to straighten him out. Declining a present that appears to have strings attached is a healthy way to set boundaries.
- Look out for the control freak, someone who insists on his

way and ignores your likes and dislikes. If he shows contempt for your tastes in restaurants, movies, and music, he may also have little regard for your physical boundaries.

- Beware of the person who tries to isolate you from your other friends and your family or who constantly bad-mouths them. If he is extremely possessive and wants you all to himself, chances are he will eventually want all of you sexually, as well.

- Steer clear of guys who tell raunchy jokes, listen to sexually explicit music, enjoy pornography, or make degrading comments about women. They have a diseased attitude about women and sexuality, and don't belong in your life.

- Don't waste your time with anyone who does not accept your limits; who begs, pleads, and haggles for physical contact; or who trots out worn and pathetic lines such as, "If you loved me, you'd do it," or, "Trust me." Anyone who pressures you for sexual favors is a loser and an abuser and most certainly doesn't love you.

How can I be proactive about ensuring that my son doesn't sexually abuse someone?

Talk explicitly to your son about respect for members of the opposite sex and about sexual responsibility. Your mission is to embed some very important values deeply into his mind and heart, not only for the teen years but for the rest of his life:

- *Never become a sexual predator.* A male who specifically sets out to maneuver women into sexual encounters might be called a "player," but he's basically a jerk. If and when you see this behavior depicted in a movie or TV program or displayed by someone you know, let your son know that this is no way to treat a woman.

- *Never push a woman's physical boundaries.* If she says no to anything, even holding hands, that statement is final and not to be questioned.

- *Respect and maintain a woman's body, integrity, and future, even if she is inviting intimacy.* Without question, one of the most difficult challenges for a healthy teenage male is holding his ground when a desirable female flashes a bright and explicit green light. *Talk through this situation, including what he might say and how to walk away from this situation immediately.* It is important that he not be flustered or embarrassed and that he be able to decline the invitation in a way that expresses a desire to protect both his own and her health and future.

- *Approach any activity or relationship with the opposite sex with the intention of enhancing the other person's life rather than leaving a wake of regrets.* Thinking in terms of protecting the other person's long-term well-being instead of merely satisfying immediate needs or desires is a sign of maturity. Some thoughtful conversations between parents and sons can help establish these grown-up attitudes.

What do I do if my daughter is sexually assaulted?

Even when appropriate precautions have been taken, it is still possible that your daughter could be the victim of a sexual assault. As unpleasant as it may be to discuss this topic, she should know what (and what not) to do if this occurs, whether the attacker is an acquaintance or a stranger.

First, she should get to a safe place as quickly as possible and contact a family member and the police *immediately*. In the emotional aftermath of an assault, the urge to deny what has happened may cause a victim to wait days or weeks to report it. But doing so reduces her credibility and makes prosecution of the attacker more difficult. Reporting the assault right away can help her regain a sense of control, obtain proper medical care, and guarantee personal safety. Furthermore, it is important that all physical evidence of the attack be preserved. She should not shower, bathe, douche, or even change clothes, even though it is normal for a woman to feel an overwhelming urge to rid herself of every trace of the attack.

Because of embarrassment, fear of reprisal, or apprehension over dealing with police, doctors, and attorneys, the majority of sexual assaults go unreported. The attacker has assumed that he could have his way without any consequences, and he must not be allowed that unjust satisfaction. He has committed a serious crime and deserves punishment for it. Furthermore, most rapists are repeat offenders, and taking action may help prevent someone else from being assaulted.

The officers who take the report will need to ask about specific details of the rape that may be painful to answer but are necessary for proper documentation of the crime. It is important that your daughter be completely honest and candid about what happened, even if she feels she made a mistake or even violated her own moral standards prior to the rape. If her story changes later on, the case against the attacker will be weakened.

The police will advise that a medical evaluation be carried out, even if your daughter does not believe she was injured. A thorough examination is necessary to assess her physical condition, to collect important evidence, and to provide counseling regarding the possibility of pregnancy or sexually transmitted infection. This should be done in a hospital emergency room where the physicians and staff are equipped to deal with rape victims or in a rape treatment center (assuming its services include an appropriate medical evaluation).

As with the police report, parts of this examination will be difficult and uncomfortable, especially if your daughter has not had a pelvic exam before. But cooperation with the physician and nurses is important, and the temporary discomfort will be worth the long-term benefits of proper medical care.

Finally, your daughter should receive counseling from an individual qualified to deal with the impact of the rape experience on her life. This event cannot be ignored and will not be forgotten. She will need both time and support to recover from the physical, emotional, and spiritual aftereffects of a sexual assault. Many powerful emotions must be sorted out, including guilt or mistaken feelings of blame.

It is important that your own anger and frustration not boil over and cause more damage. This is not the time for comments such as "I told you so" or "How could you have let this happen?" Even if your daughter used extremely poor judgment or flatly disobeyed your explicit instructions, she in no way "asked for" or deserved a sexual assault. She will need your help to rebuild her sense of dignity and worth. Without this important repair work, she will be vulnerable to sexual pressure and abuse in the future.

What do I do if my son is sexually assaulted?

The vast majority of information and advisories regarding rape are directed toward females, who are most commonly—but not exclusively—the victims of sexual assault. In a less frequent (but no less serious) situation, an adolescent or young adult male may be the sexual target of one or more other men. Should this happen to your son, you will need to muster all the same strength and support you would offer a daughter who had been attacked.

In particular, it is critical that appropriate medical assessment, evidence collection, preventive measures for sexually transmitted infections, and counseling be provided in a timely fashion, just as in the case of a female victim. If possible, the perpetrator(s) should be identified, arrested, and prosecuted. Even if a parent learns about an assault months or years after it took place, medical care and counseling should be provided. It is particularly important that such an event not be allowed to confuse an adolescent's sense of sexual identity or integrity.

What can I do if my daughter becomes pregnant?

Before considering how you might respond to the news that your unmarried teenager is pregnant, take a brief tour of the emotions and thought processes that are likely to be swirling through her mind and heart.

Fear is an overriding emotion in nearly every teen pregnancy. "I can't tell my parents. They'll kill me!" "How can I finish school when I'm pregnant?" "My boyfriend will bail if I don't have an abortion." The adolescent with a crisis pregnancy probably sees nothing but loss on the horizon—loss of love, time, education, and physical health. Fear of one or more of these losses propels most of her other responses.

Denial is common, especially during the early weeks of pregnancy when the only indication might be one or more missed periods, a little fatigue, possibly some nausea, or even a positive pregnancy test. The longing for things to be the way they were may delay acknowledging the problem and seeking appropriate help for weeks or even months.

Ambivalence about being pregnant may cause fluctuating emotions. One day the only solution may appear to be an abortion, while the next the prospect of a cuddly baby may seem appealing. Time spent with a friend's crying newborn may jolt the emotions in yet another direction. Indecision and apparent lack of direction in such an overwhelming situation are common.

When a pregnancy results from the violation of moral values held since childhood, an adolescent will usually feel ashamed and worthless. Her growing abdomen becomes a constant reminder of her failure.

Pressure to have an abortion may come from several directions. A teenager may be weighing what appears to be a dismal future of hardship and remorse against a quick and relatively inexpensive procedure. "No one needs to know, and I can get on with my life." A boyfriend (who may be dealing with his own fear and guilt, along with concerns about future financial responsibilities) may exert considerable pressure to abort, even offering to pay the bill. He may also threaten to bail out of the relationship if the pregnancy continues. Some parents, worried about their daughter's future or perhaps their own reputation in the community (or even the prospect of being responsible for the actual child rearing), may also find abortion attractive.

Some unmarried teenage girls see their pregnancy unrealistically as an escape from a difficult and unpleasant home situation. They may envision a baby as a snuggly companion who will require roughly the same amount of care as a new puppy, not realizing the amount of energy a newborn will require without giving much in return (especially during the first few weeks). Teens with this mind-set need to adjust their expectations of child rearing—not to drive them to abort but to help them make more appropriate plans. If adoption is not chosen as a solution, some careful groundwork should be laid to prevent serious disappointment and even the mother's abuse of the baby.

What can I do if my son is involved in a pregnancy?

If your son has had a sexual relationship from which a pregnancy has resulted, remember that he will probably be experiencing many of the same emotions as his girlfriend, including fear, guilt, and ambivalence. In addition, he will feel considerable conflict and confusion over the role he should play.

Usually, the relationship with the mother-to-be has not, until this point, involved any long-range plans. Now he must make a decision about the level of commitment he intends to assume, and the issues are significant. What does he owe this young woman?

Can he walk away from this situation? Should he make a lifelong commitment to her because of this unplanned pregnancy?

He does not bear the biological consequences, of course, and the mother of the baby has the legal right to have an abortion or carry the pregnancy to term with or without his input. This may leave him with the impression that he has no control over the unplanned pregnancy and therefore no responsibility for it. As his parents, you are one step further removed from the situation and may have similar questions about the role you should play.

Above all, your son will need encouragement and guidance to assume the appropriate level of responsibility for his role in the pregnancy. He should not be allowed to abandon his girlfriend with a cavalier, hit-and-run attitude. "It's her problem now" or "She should have protected herself" or even "She should just get an abortion" are shallow and disrespectful responses to a serious situation. Pushing for a quick marriage may seem honorable, but is probably unwise. Teenage matrimony carries with it very short odds of long-term success, and the combination of immaturity, lack of resources, and the intense demands of a newborn baby will usually strain an adolescent relationship to the breaking point.

In a best-case scenario, the families of both participants will cooperate to find a productive balance among several tasks: facing the consequences of the sexual relationship, accountability of teens to the adults in both families, short-term and long-term planning, and mature decision making.

Your son will need encouragement to acknowledge his responsibility to the girl's family and to accept with humility their response, whether it is measured or angry. You and your son may face the possibility that the other family will choose to deal with the pregnancy on their own, even if you are willing to participate in the process. And if that decision includes forbidding your son to have further contact with someone about whom he cares very deeply, he will have to find the strength to abide by the other parents' wishes. If he is allowed to continue his relationship with the mother-to-be and support her when the going gets tough, clear ground rules (including abstaining from further sexual contact) will need to be established and respected.

Having a pregnant girlfriend is tough and painful. But it also can be an opportunity for your son to mature, to find out what he is made of. In the long run, the pregnant adolescent girl isn't the only one who has to make important choices.

What if my child is unsure about his sexual orientation?

Few parenting concerns during adolescence generate as much emotional turbulence as the possibility that one's child might have a homosexual orientation. For many parents, especially those deeply committed to traditional values, the thought of a child becoming involved in homosexual relationships raises unsettling moral questions. For some, reactions to homosexuality extend into the darker emotions of hatred and loathing.

In contrast, many influential voices in media, government, and health care promote the unproven notion that sexual orientation is inborn and unchangeable. In their view, if your child is destined to be attracted to members of the same sex, nothing can or should be done about it other than to accept it. Gay and lesbian activists proclaim that teens who feel same-sex inclinations should explore, embrace, and celebrate their homosexual identity and that their parents should celebrate it along with them.

The vast majority of parents, while neither hating homosexual individuals nor applauding homosexuality, deeply desire to see their teens eventually bear and rear children. They anticipate the joys of watching the next generation's courtships, marriages, and family lives. Therefore, contemplating a child's involvement in homosexual acts and in unconventional relationships for decades into the future is enough to provoke considerable concern, if not ongoing insomnia.

What should you do if your adolescent's sexual orientation is uncertain or if she has had one or more homosexual experiences?

Don't assume that characteristics that fall outside your gender expectations indicate homosexual tendencies. A boy who has a slight build and prefers painting over pitching or fabrics over football may disappoint a father who envisioned bringing up a burly, athletic hero. A daughter who isn't shapely or petite and who excels at basketball rather than ballet may not fulfill a mother's expectations of magazine-cover femininity. But both need unconditional affirmation of their worth from parents who accept and encourage their particular strengths as appropriate.

What may drive a teenager toward same-gender sexuality is ongoing rejection from parents or peers. Cutting remarks about a teenager's size, shape, or other attributes merely reinforce the idea that "I'm different from everyone else." If genuine acceptance is eventually offered by someone with a homosexual orientation, the teenager may conclude, "I'm different, so that must mean I'm gay—and furthermore, I've always been this way."

Remember that teens may feel transient confusion about sexual identity, especially if they have had a sexual experience with someone of the same gender. Whether as a phase of rebellion and experimentation or as the result of sexual abuse in childhood, an adolescent may have one or more same-sex encounters, which may raise questions about his ultimate sexual destination. It is therefore important for teens who have had such experiences to receive appropriate counseling that (among other things) will clarify the fact that these events have not destined them to a lifelong homosexual orientation.

If you discover that your child has had one or more homo-sexual encounters, whether coerced or voluntary, you need to remain his strongest ally. Adolescents who have suffered sexual abuse need to know that what happened was not their fault and that their parents are not in any way ashamed of them. They will need comfort, reassurance that their physical boundaries are now secure, and time to sort out their experiences, both with their parents (which will be very uncomfortable) and with a professional counselor. It is crucial that the damage done by an abuser to a child's sexual identity and sense of self-worth be contained.

If the activities involved one or more peers and were not the result of coercion, your response should parallel what was outlined in connection with premarital heterosexual activity. You will need to make a particular effort to maintain a balance between taking a clear stand for moral principles and demonstrating that you and your adolescent are still on the same team. Harsh expressions of revulsion and condemnation are counterproductive, will probably confirm your teenager's feelings of alienation, and may very well provoke more of the same behavior. At the same time, a resigned and passive nonresponse ("Nothing can be done about this, so I might as well get used to it") squanders an opportunity to bring about change. As with other early and mid-adolescent sexual activity, conversation and counseling with someone who shares your values is in order.

You must commit to patience, prayer, and perseverance. You may shed rivers of tears, but you must not allow animosity or bitterness to take root in your emotions. Most of all, you will need generous amounts of wisdom, because you may be the only voice expressing love while encouraging your child to begin the difficult process of disengaging from ongoing homosexual behavior. A resource you may find very helpful is Love Won Out, sponsored by Exodus International (www.exodusinternational.org).

CHAPTER 5

TOBACCO, ALCOHOL, AND DRUG ABUSE: CURBING THE EPIDEMIC

A man is a slave to whatever has mastered him.

2 PETER 2:19

GENERATIONS AGO, our ancestors watched in horror as bubonic plague, diphtheria, smallpox, and other lethal epidemics swept through their towns and families, taking rich and poor alike to the grave. Today the consumption of alcohol, tobacco, and a host of addicting drugs has become a modern-day plague ravaging many of our youngest citizens.

Like the scourges of old, the drug epidemic spreads without regard to economic, racial, geographic, educational, religious, or family boundaries. More recently, it has become particularly aggressive among preteen children, dipping freely into the primary grades for new consumers. While we all should work and pray toward ending this blight in our nation and our communities, we must ultimately be concerned about preventing it from moving across our own doorsteps.

No child will automatically be immune from the drug epidemic.

You must work diligently over the years to "drug proof" your children. This project involves a number of tasks that cannot be tackled haphazardly. These encompass some basic knowledge about substance abuse, preventive messages, awareness of possible problems in your—yes, even *your*—kids, and, if needed, intervention.

Why do kids start and continue using drugs?

Four factors set the stage for adolescent drug use:

- *Attitudes of parents toward tobacco, alcohol, and other substances.* Children learn from what they experience. Smoking, drinking, and other drug-related behaviors among parents will usually be duplicated by their children.
- *Attractiveness of drugs.* Smoking and drinking are widely promoted as habits enjoyed by sophisticated, fun-loving, attractive, and sexy people—what most teens long to become. Illegal drugs are "advertised" by those using them in an adolescent's peer group.
- *The high induced by drugs.* If drug use weren't pleasurable, it would be relatively easy to keep your teenagers away from harmful substances. But the reality is that many adolescents enjoy the way they feel on drugs—at least for a while.
- *Availability of drugs.* Finding drugs is not difficult for teenagers in most communities, but tougher local standards can help keep drugs out of less-determined hands.

Once the stage is set, the following factors exert a more direct influence on who will and who won't try drugs. The consequences of early experiences (whether pleasant or disagreeable), the drug used, and one's genetic predisposition will determine whether a problem is nipped in the bud or blossoms into addiction.

Peer pressure. Peers play a huge role at each stage of an adolescent's drug experience—whether resisting them, experimenting, becoming a user, or confronting withdrawal and recovery. The need for peer acceptance is especially strong during the early adolescent years and can override (or at least seriously challenge) the most earnest commitments. "Just say no" may not mean a whole lot when smoking, drinking, or taking drugs determines who is included in highly esteemed ranks of the social circle.

There are three important implications to the association between peers and drug use:

- It is important that kids find their niche in the right peer group, among friends who are not only committed to positive values (including drug-free lifestyles), but who are also involved in worthwhile and enjoyable pursuits.
- You may have to intervene if your adolescent (especially in the early teen years) is hanging out with the wrong crowd.
- Teenagers with a healthy, stable identity and an appropriate sense of independence will be more resistant to peer pressure. (See page 49.)

Curiosity. Unless your family lives in total isolation, your child will be aware of smoking, alcohol, and drug use well before adolescence from discussions at school, watching TV and movies, or direct observation. Some curiosity is inevitable: What do these things feel like? Whether this leads to sampling, and whether an experiment progresses to addiction, will depend on the individual's mind-set and physical response.

Thrill seeking. To some degree, we all have a desire for excitement, which propels us toward all kinds of thrill-seeking activities: extreme sports, roller coasters, movies (where sights and sounds are "bigger than life"), fireworks displays, and so on. Some of these are riskier than others, but none requires chemical altera-tion of the senses to be satisfying. Unfortunately, many teenagers seek drug experiences to produce thrills that normal conscious-ness can't duplicate.

Rebellion. Wayward teens may engage in smoking, drinking, and drug use as a show of "independence" from family norms and values.

Escape from life/relief from pain. This is often the driving force in drug use. If everyday life seems boring, meaningless, oppres-sive, or painful (physically or emotionally), alcohol and drugs may appear to offer a powerful time-out. The strongest resistance to drug abuse, therefore, arises from an ongoing sense of joy and contentment that transcends circumstances. These attitudes are usually acquired, not inborn. Early positive experiences in the family and an active, wide-awake relationship with God play the most important roles in molding such attitudes.

Why is adolescent smoking such a major concern?

No drug habit has a greater negative impact on our national health than tobacco, which is implicated in more than 400,000 deaths in the United States each year. The list of disorders caused or aggra-vated by tobacco is staggering. Among these diseases are cancers of the lungs, mouth, vocal cords, and other organs; chronic lung disease; asthma; ulcers; and clogging of the vessels that sup-ply blood to the heart and other organs, causing heart attacks, strokes, amputations, and premature deaths. Babies and children who breathe smokers' exhaust at home are at risk for respiratory infections, asthma, and sudden infant death syndrome (SIDS). The vast majority of diseases related to tobacco take their toll later in life after subjects have had years of exposure.

Nicotine is extremely addictive. A typical cigarette contains only about one milligram (mg) of nicotine, but smoking sends it from the lungs into the bloodstream with remarkable efficiency, rivaling that of an injection directly into the veins. (A 60 mg dose of nicotine, if consumed all at once, would be lethal.) Each cigarette delivers several hits of nicotine that stimulate receptors in the brain, producing a unique combination of relaxation and alertness. Furthermore, as habitual smokers can attest, withdrawal is associated with unpleasant physical and psychological symptoms. The result is a physiological reward pattern that frequently becomes a compulsion—*especially when smoking begins at an early age*.

Almost every long-term smoker picks up the habit during adolescence. More than 80 percent of adult smokers initiated their habit before the age of eighteen.[11] As of 2009, 17 percent of high school students identified themselves as current smokers, although rates have gradually declined since 1997.[12] Every day, nearly four thousand children younger than eighteen try their first cigarette, and of these nearly one in four will become regular smokers.[13] The American Lung Association estimates that more than 6.4 million children alive today will die prematurely because of a decision to try smoking before they reach adulthood.[14]

Cigarettes keep very bad company. Smoking is associated with significantly poorer school performance and a higher likelihood of sexual activity. Because the use of alcohol and marijuana is significantly greater among adolescent smokers, tobacco is identified as a gateway drug—one that increases the odds that a teen will begin using even more dangerous substances. A 2010 survey conducted by the Substance Abuse and Mental Health Service (SAMHSA) found that the rate of current illicit drug use was more than eight times higher among adolescents twelve to seventeen who smoked cigarettes in the past month (52.9 percent), compared with those who did not smoke cigarettes in the previous month (6.2 percent).[15]

It is the last of these points that should sound the alarm for parents of adolescent smokers.

Smokeless (chewing and snuffing) tobacco, which has been made highly visible (and glamorized to some degree) by users who are professional athletes, is not a safe alternative to cigarettes. The only good news about the use of smokeless tobacco among teens is that it has been decreasing following a peak in the mid-1990s. Chewing tobacco is clearly associated with damage to the gingiva (the soft tissues surrounding the teeth) and with aggressive cancers of the mouth. Furthermore, both chewing and snuffing deliver powerful jolts of nicotine. A typical dose of snuff contains more than twice the amount of nicotine in a cigarette, and a wad of chewing tobacco contains fifteen times that amount. It's no surprise that addiction to these substances is very common, as are withdrawal symptoms when use is stopped.

What are the harmful effects of alcohol?

Alcohol use by those under twenty-one is illegal in all fifty states for several good reasons. Alcohol causes more deaths among teens than any other illicit substance. It is involved in approximately half of all automobile crashes involving teenagers (the leading cause of death in this age-group), and it frequently plays a role in adolescent deaths from other causes, including homicides, suicides, drownings, and motorcycle and bicycle accidents. It is also linked to two out of three sexual assaults and date rapes, and it plays a prominent role in high-risk sex among the young.

To say that putting alcohol into a young body frequently leads to reckless, dangerous, violent, and lethal outcomes is not breaking news. The human brain undergoes important transformations during adolescence and is more vulnerable to damage from alcohol before age twenty-one than at any time later in life. The underage drinker who is "sowing wild oats" may in fact be reaping long-term—or even lifelong—problems with learning and relationships.

A number of underage drinkers develop full-blown alcohol addiction and struggle with it for years. Ironically, the person who prides himself on the ability to "hold his liquor" is at the greatest risk for alcoholism. If large quantities of alcohol must be consumed to produce intoxication, it demonstrates a tolerance for alcohol—something all alcoholics have in common—and addiction is likely to develop. Tolerance of alcohol and the risk of addiction are thought to be genetically predisposed and usually run in families. Teens with family members who have had alcohol-abuse problems must be warned that they are at higher risk for becoming addicted to alcohol if they ever start drinking.

What is marijuana?

Marijuana is a shredded mix of various parts (leaves, stems, seeds, flowers) of the hemp plant *Cannabis sativa*. Hashish (the Arabic word for hemp) is the sticky resin of the female plant flowers, containing an average of 3.6 percent (or as much as 28 percent) tetrahydrocannabinol (THC), its main mood-altering chemical, along with four hundred other assorted compounds. Marijuana is the most commonly used illegal drug in the United States.

How it is used. Marijuana is most commonly smoked, whether rolled into a cigarette, packed into a pipe, or stuffed into a cigar from which tobacco has been removed. Crack cocaine or other dangerous drugs may be added to the mix to be smoked, with or without the user's knowledge, sometimes with unpleasant results. Marijuana can also be added to foods or drinks (or even brewed as tea), though much more THC is delivered to the brain when the drug is inhaled. When smoked, its effects are felt almost immediately and typically last one to three hours. In food or drink, effects are delayed by thirty to sixty minutes, but may last as long as four hours.

Health risks. The casual attitudes about marijuana in our culture and media over the past four decades would suggest that smoking marijuana is no more than a harmless diversion. But the opposite is true: Marijuana smoke is more irritating to the mouth, throat, airway, and lungs than tobacco smoke, and it contains 50 to 70 percent more cancer-provoking hydrocarbons. The tendency to inhale deeply and hold one's breath while smoking aggravates this tendency. Long-term marijuana smokers, like their tobacco-puffing counterparts, are thus at higher risk for developing not only chronic lung disease but also cancer of the upper respiratory tract and lungs.

Other consequences. Marijuana's greatest drawback, especially in light of its widespread use among the young, is that it impairs intellectual function—concentration, memory, and judgment—as well as motor skills. During the teen years, one should be learning how to think and act more maturely, but frequent marijuana use can derail that process. Short-term fallout can include injuries and death from motor-vehicle accidents or other trauma, as well as sexual misadventures resulting from loss of inhibition and rational thinking. A number of research studies have demonstrated that impairment of memory, learning, and concentration continues for days or weeks after the immediate effects of the drug wear off.

Long-term users are known for an amotivational syndrome in which goals and self-discipline (especially in school and work performance) literally go up in smoke. One study demonstrated lower scores on standardized verbal and mathematical tests among twelfth-grade marijuana smokers compared to their nonsmoking peers, even though the two groups had performed equally well during the fourth grade. Other research has associated marijuana use with overall poorer job performance, including increased tardiness, absenteeism, accidents, and workers' compensation claims.

Finally, marijuana keeps very bad company. For adolescents

and young adults alike, it can be a gateway drug, introducing them to the world of illegal drugs and the criminals who produce and distribute them.

Though marijuana is not widely perceived as highly addictive, some long-term users continue to smoke it compulsively even though it is clearly having a negative impact on school, work, and relationships. Long-term regular users who quit may experience anxiety, irritability, and sleeplessness.

What are inhalants?

Three types of products are inhaled by young thrill seekers:

- *Solvents* or solvent-containing products, such as paint thinner, lacquers, degreasers, model glue, contact cement, gasoline, felt-tip marker fluid, and dozens of other volatile products. These can have mind-altering effects if inhaled deeply.
- *Aerosols* that contain solvents and propellants, such as hair sprays, deodorants, and spray paint.
- *Gases* present in household products such as whipping-cream dispensers, butane lighters, and propane tanks.

Inhalant use typically starts in childhood or early adolescence. The age of peak use is typically twelve to fourteen, with first experiences occurring as early as six to eight years of age.

How they are used. Solvents, gases, or aerosols are inhaled through the nose (sniffing) or the mouth (huffing), either directly from the container, from plastic bags containing the fumes and held over the mouth and nose, or from a cloth that has been sprayed or saturated with the material.

Health risks. Given the huge variety of toxins that are being abused through inhalation, it should come as little surprise that a host of serious medical consequences have been observed. A number of products can be lethal during or after a single use. One disastrous consequence known as *sudden sniffing death syndrome* can occur in a previously healthy user, especially when butane, propane, or aerosols are inhaled. (This may result from an increased sensitivity of the heart muscle, and it is possible that an abrupt adrenaline surge in response to being startled can provoke a lethal irregular heart rhythm.) Users can also die by asphyxiation when the inhaled substance interferes with oxygen exchange within the lungs, or by suffocation from a plastic bag pulled over the head.

The most serious by-product of chronic inhalant use is permanent damage to the brain and nervous system, causing loss of intellectual function and coordination. Depending on chemical structure and the number and intensity of exposures, inhaled substances can also damage the tissues of other internal organs. Toluene, for example, found in glue, spray paint, and gasoline, can cause brain damage (including actual loss of tissue), disturbances of gait (walking) and coordination, vision and hearing loss, and injury to the liver or kidneys.

Other consequences. Like other drug users, inhalant abusers may display erratic behavior, poor self-care, and declining school performance. Parents may notice specific clues such as the aroma of the inhalant (which can persist in the breath for several hours), stains and odors in clothes, and an unusual stash of products (such as gasoline or aerosol cans) in a child's room. An adult who discovers children or adolescents in the act of inhaling should avoid surprise tactics or a sudden confrontation that might cause a startle reflex, since this could precipitate a dangerous heart-rhythm disturbance.

What are steroids?

Competitive athletes and bodybuilders of both sexes may be tempted to boost their physical prowess by using *anabolic steroids*. These compounds are chemically distinct from *corticosteroids* (such as prednisone) prescribed by physicians to treat allergic reactions, asthma, and many other conditions. Though some forms of anabolic steroids are available to treat specific medical problems, prescribing them for athletic or bodybuilding purposes is illegal.

How they are used. Anabolic steroids are readily available to teens through underground sources. Abusers of these drugs may "stack" them (take more than one type at once) or utilize "pyramiding" (increasing the dose, sometimes to massive levels, over time). They can be swallowed, injected, or applied to the skin.

Signs of abuse. Aggressive behavior, impaired judgment, abuse of alcohol and other drugs, and in some cases, significant psychiatric disturbances, including psychosis (losing touch with reality), may be associated with the use of anabolic steroids.

Health risks. Male users may develop acne, reduction in size and function of the testicles, impotence, purplish skin marks called *striae*, and male-pattern baldness. Women risk developing a permanently low-pitched voice, thinning hair around the temples, enlargement of the clitoris, striae, and increased facial hair. Adolescent users may retard their growth or end it prematurely, resulting in a shorter stature than they would have otherwise attained. All users risk liver disease, elevated blood pressure, and heart disease.

Treatment options. School programs are now more actively addressing the issues surrounding steroid abuse. Adolescent steroid abuse should be taken as seriously as any other illicit drug problem. A medical evaluation and ongoing counseling should be carried out to address dependence, withdrawal symptoms, and the underlying causes of this drug-seeking behavior.

What about prescription and nonprescription drug abuse?

Tobacco, alcohol, and illegal drugs aren't the only potential chemical traps that can snare teens and children. Many seek mind-altering experiences from the family medicine cabinet, sometimes with shocking—and at times lethal—abandon.

The most widely abused prescription drugs are

- *Opiates*: painkillers related to morphine, most commonly *hydrocodone* combined with acetaminophen (Vicodin, Norco, and other brands and generics) and *oxycodone* (Percodan, Percocet, OxyContin, and other brands). OxyContin, a potent, time-released medication intended for serious chronic pain problems (such as those associated with cancer), has been abused by teens who may crush pills designed to be taken whole—thus allowing a sudden and potentially dangerous rush of medication into the bloodstream.[16]

- *Anxiety-reducing drugs*: also known as *anxiolytic* drugs, or by the more familiar but less specific term *tranquilizers*. Most of these drugs are in the family known as *benzodiazepines*, which, when used properly, are effective for controlling acute or chronic anxiety. In an overdose, especially when combined with other sedating drugs or alcohol, they can cause dramatic and sometimes fatal suppression of one's ability to breathe. Widely used benzodiazepines include alprazolam (Xanax), lorazepam (Ativan), clonazepam (Klonopin), and diazepam (Valium).

- *Stimulants*: medications that are widely used to treat attention deficit/hyperactivity disorder (ADHD), primarily variations on *methylphenidate* (Ritalin, Concerta, Metadate, and others) and *dextroamphetamine* (Dexedrine, Adderall, and others). When prescribed for the right individual and carefully monitored, these medications can be very useful, but some teens share them with (or sell them to) friends. Taking an excessive dose of a stimulant (especially when combined with other drugs such as those found in decongestant cold tablets) can provoke a variety of dangerous medical complications, including an irregular heart rhythm, elevated blood pressure, or lethal seizures.

Currently, the most widely abused nonprescription medication is *dextromethorphan*, a cough suppressant (often denoted by the letters *DM* in a product's name) found in more than 120 different preparations and intended to relieve cough and cold symptoms. When taken in the appropriate amounts (as found on the product packaging or as prescribed by a physician), dextromethorphan has no psychological effects. At much higher doses, however—what abusers call "robodosing" or "robotripping," a slang reference to the familiar cough syrup Robitussin—dextromethorphan can cause alterations in consciousness that can range from euphoric to highly unpleasant. (Some of these effects may be altered by other substances in the particular dextromethorphan-containing medication that is being abused, or by alcohol and other drugs taken at the same time.)

What can I do to prevent my child's abuse of legal drugs?

The drug-proofing strategies described later (starting on page 145) certainly apply here. In addition, while talking to your kids about tobacco, alcohol, and illegal drugs, you might also include some serious family "public service announcements" about the dangers of misusing prescription and nonprescription drugs. Also, think carefully about where your family's medications are stored—all drugs should be out of plain sight, perhaps hidden or even kept in a locked drawer. Also, keep careful tabs on the status of any commonly abused drugs that have been acquired by *anyone* in the family for a legitimate purpose. In particular, if your child or teenager is taking medications for ADHD, anxiety, or pain relief, with rare exception you should be the one dispensing them on a day-to-day basis. Even if you can count on your son or daughter to use them responsibly, it's important to protect friends who might be tempted by a prescription bottle sitting on the counter.

What are "club drugs"?

A number of unrelated substances have been grouped under this title because they are used by teenagers and young adults at dance clubs and bars, particularly at raves and trances—all-night dance parties held in clubs, warehouses, or even outdoors, for groups ranging from a few hundred to several thousand. While rave and trance culture is focused primarily on the driving music and the physical and emotional release of dancing for hours with an exuberant crowd, there are many who try to enhance the experience with one or more drugs, sometimes with disastrous results.

The most common club drugs include MDMA (Ecstasy) and the "date-rape drugs" Rohypnol and gamma hydroxybutyrate (GHB). Methamphetamine, a relative of MDMA that has been an abused drug for many years, often shows up at the rave scene as well. Obviously, this cast of characters is subject to change without notice. To complicate matters, club drugs are often combined with one another, with alcohol, and with other drugs. The exact ingredients in the concoctions for sale at an all-night party, not to mention the presence of possible contaminants, are highly unpredictable—and so is the range of possible effects. Teens and young adults who have had an earful of warnings about "hard stuff" such as heroin and cocaine may feel that club drugs are a safer bet. But the odds are much worse than they imagine, and losing the bet can have far-reaching consequences. Those interested in staying current on this phenomenon may get updates at www.clubdrugs .org, a service of the National Institute on Drug Abuse.

What is Ecstasy?

MDMA is a synthetic drug with a chemical structure resembling both methamphetamine (a stimulant) and mescaline (a hallucinogen). Originally intended to be an appetite suppressant, MDMA was used in psychotherapy during the 1970s to help individuals open up and discuss their emotions. This practice was discontinued in the mid-1980s, when researchers found that MDMA causes brain damage in animals.

How it is used. MDMA is nearly always swallowed as a pill, although more adventurous (and foolhardy) individuals may crush pills and then snort the powder or inject a solution containing it. Occasionally MDMA is taken in suppository form.

Health risks. Like other stimulants, MDMA can raise the pulse and blood pressure, and may interfere with temperature regulation. In hot, stuffy, tightly packed club settings, the combination of MDMA and the ongoing intense exertion of dancing can lead to *hyperthermia*, a marked increase in body temperature, which in turn can cause muscle breakdown, kidney failure, and other catastrophic effects. Also, as is typical with stimulants, MDMA use can provoke anxiety, headache, irritability, depression, insomnia, and paranoia—just the opposite of the good feelings that are its primary appeal. Users may also experience significant depression as a withdrawal effect just two days after the last dose.

Perhaps the most worrisome aspect of MDMA use is the finding that it causes long-term brain damage in animals and produces changes in brain scans (using positron-emission tomography) in humans. Some research suggests MDMA users score more poorly on memory tests than their nonusing counterparts, but whether such changes are permanent is unknown.

What are "date-rape drugs"?

The drugs *Rohypnol* and *gamma hydroxybutyrate (GHB)* are predator tools. Accounts of sexual predators using them to incapacitate victims led Congress to pass the Drug-Induced Rape Prevention and Punishment Act of 1996, increasing federal penalties for the use of any controlled substance in a sexual assault.

Rohypnol was originally introduced as a sleeping aid in Europe in the 1970s, but it was found to cause short-term loss of memory and profound drowsiness, especially when mixed with alcohol. It has never been approved for use in the United States, but it is produced and legally available in Europe and Latin America.

Until the early 1990s, GHB was sold in health-food stores and touted as an aid for weight reduction and bodybuilding. It is in fact a central nervous system depressant, especially when mixed with alcohol.

How they are used. Both drugs are taken orally: Rohypnol is taken as a pill or ground into powder; GHB, as a powder or liquid. Both are colorless, tasteless, and odorless.

Health risks. Long-term users of Rohypnol are likely to develop physical and psychological dependence, and may have withdrawal symptoms (including an increased risk for seizures) when the drug is stopped. Depending on dose and other drugs being taken, GHB's sedative effects can be extreme, leading to unconsciousness, coma, and even death. By far the most grievous damage related to these drugs, however, is the fallout from a sexual assault: physical and emotional trauma, as well as the possibility of pregnancy or a sexually transmitted infection.

What is methamphetamine?

A derivative of amphetamine and chemically similar in some respects to MDMA, methamphetamine is a potent central nervous system stimulant. When first synthesized, it was used as a nasal decongestant and asthma treatment. Today, it is still prescribed occasionally to treat narcolepsy (a disorder in which an individual suddenly falls asleep without warning) and ADHD. Unfortunately, it is relatively easy to manufacture in home laboratories using store-bought ingredients, making it the most commonly synthesized illegal drug in the United States.

How it is used. Methamphetamine is taken in tablet form, dissolved in water or alcohol, smoked, snorted, or injected. Yaba, a tablet containing methamphetamine and caffeine, has been popular in Southeast Asia and has begun to appear in Asian communities on the West Coast.

Health risks. Methamphetamine stimulates not only the nervous system but also the rest of the body, raising the pulse rate (and the likelihood of irregular heart rhythms), blood pressure, and body temperature. Heart attack, stroke, hyperthermia (dangerously elevated body temperature), seizures, and death are all possible consequences. Users who inject methamphetamine, like users of any drug shot into a vein, run the risk of acquiring HIV/AIDS and hepatitis B or C from shared needles or other equipment, not to mention bacterial infections of the skin, bone, or heart.

Long-term use is likely to lead not only to addiction, but also to induce long-term or even permanent changes in the central nervous system. (Some evidence suggests that damage to nerve endings in the brain may occur after a single dose.) Intense emotional and behavioral turbulence—agitation, anxiety, insomnia, and violent behavior—are not uncommon. Psychosis, with delusions, hallucinations, and paranoia (including homicidal or suicidal thoughts), can result.

Other consequences. Depression, fatigue, anxiety, and an intense craving for another dose occur when the high wears off. Methamphetamine users may embark on a desperate run in order to override their tolerance for the drug, injecting large quantities every few hours over several days in a sleepless binge.

What is cocaine?

Cocaine, the most powerful stimulant occurring in nature, is one of the most addictive drugs on the street and in many ways the most dangerous. Coca leaves, the source of cocaine, grow in the highlands of the Andes in South America, primarily in Colombia, Bolivia, and Peru. In the late 1800s, pure cocaine hydrochloride was extracted from coca leaves and found to be useful in medical procedures involving the nose and eyes because of its ability to reduce pain and constrict blood vessels. In crack cocaine (also called freebase), the hydrochloride has been removed, creating a form of the drug that can be smoked. The crackling sound that occurs when cocaine is heated during this preparation gives the final product its name.

Note: The *coca* bush bears no relation to the tropical *cacao* tree, from which we obtain chocolate and cocoa.

How it is used. Cocaine is nearly always inhaled (snorted), entering the bloodstream via the inner linings of the nose; injected into a vein; or smoked. When inhaled, its high lasts about ten to fifteen minutes—much shorter than that seen with methamphetamine. When injected or smoked, the effects are felt immediately but may last only a few minutes. Cocaine is also injected along with heroin (a combination known as a speedball, among other names), smoked with tobacco or marijuana, or combined with virtually any other mind-altering drug. Powdered cocaine may be diluted with cornstarch, talcum, or sugar.

Health risks. There are many, and they're serious. Cocaine's powerful jolt to the central nervous system also triggers a rapid heart rate, constricted blood vessels, and elevated blood pressure. Even in young, well-conditioned bodies, these events can cause stroke, seizures, or cardiac arrest. Cocaine precipitates more emergency-room visits than any other illegal drug.

All of cocaine's routes of entry into the body pose unique hazards. Snorting cocaine up the nose can lead to destruction of the septum (the structure separating the two nasal passages) and eventual collapse of the bridge of the nose. Injecting cocaine into the veins can transmit dangerous microorganisms, including the viruses that cause hepatitis and AIDS, when needles or syringes are shared with other users. Allergic reactions to injected cocaine or to one of the additives mixed with it can be severe or even fatal.

When cocaine and alcohol are used at the same time (not an uncommon event), the liver may convert them to a compound called *cocaethylene*, which is more toxic than either drug alone. According to the National Institute on Drug Abuse, cocaine and alcohol, when used together, are the two drugs most likely to result in death.

Multiple doses of cocaine taken in a binge—often involving increasing doses because tolerance has resulted in a diminishing effect—can lead to increasing restlessness, paranoia, or psychosis, complete with delusions and hallucinations.

Other consequences. When the drug wears off, cocaine users become anxious, irritable, depressed, and desperate for the next dose. Bigger and more frequent doses are needed to produce the desired effect, and the progression from first use to desperate addiction can be rapid. (With crack, addiction frequently begins with the first dose.) Money becomes important solely as a means to obtain more cocaine, and huge sums may be spent, borrowed, or stolen to buy it. Exchanges of sex for drugs enhance the spread of HIV/AIDS, hepatitis, and other infections.

What is heroin?

Heroin is the most highly addictive narcotic and the scourge of any individual, family, or neighborhood affected by it. Though by no means the most widely used illegal drug, heroin generates disproportionate medical problems, crime, and general chaos. A derivative of morphine, heroin was first synthesized in 1874 and, like cocaine, was widely used by physicians at the turn of the century before its powerful potential for addiction was recognized.

How it is used. For decades, heroin has most commonly been taken by direct injection into a vein. Because of increasing supplies of purer and cheaper heroin, however, more users now smoke or sniff it.

Health risks. As with cocaine, there are many, and they are serious, especially for users who inject it. Veins that are repeatedly invaded by needles and nonsterile materials become scarred, and bacteria accidentally shot into the bloodstream can infect heart valves, bone, and other tissues.

Heroin sold on the street doesn't go through quality control. Dealer profits are increased when the drug is diluted (or cut) with other substances such as sugar, cornstarch, powdered milk, other illegal drugs, or even strychnine (which is often used as a rodent poison). Some of these materials do not dissolve in the blood and may obstruct small arteries, leading to tissue damage in vital organs such as the lungs, liver, kidney, or brain. These damaged areas are in turn more vulnerable to bacteria introduced during injections.

Sharing needles and other paraphernalia greatly increases the risk of spreading life-threatening viral infections, including HIV/AIDS and hepatitis B and C. The Centers for Disease Control estimate that about one in ten HIV infections in the United States are transmitted this way, and that one in three young (age 18–30) intravenous drug users are infected with hepatitis C.[17] These infections can then be spread to sexual partners and from infected mothers to their babies.

The chaotic lifestyle, poor self-care, malnutrition, and general squalor that characterize the lives of hard-core addicts set them up for even more infections, such as tuberculosis, pneumonia, and skin ulcers.

Heroin users rapidly develop tolerance—bigger doses are needed to bring about a pleasurable effect—and physical dependence, such that without a steady supply of the drug, the user experiences an unpleasant withdrawal within several hours.

Variations in the quantity and purity of heroin can result in a user getting a much bigger dose than expected. Heroin overdose puts the brain into a stupor or flat-out unconsciousness and depresses respirations. If the dose is big enough, and especially if the user has ingested other sedating drugs (such as alcohol), any injection could lead to the morgue.

Like cocaine, heroin can rapidly draw a user into a full-time pursuit of the next dose and the funds necessary to acquire it. Wages (if there is a job), savings, and possessions are likely to be consumed by this addiction. Theft, dealing one or more drugs, prostitution, or simply trading sex for the next dose often become part of a grim way of life.

Other consequences. With increasing tolerance leading to bigger doses of heroin, physical dependence is virtually inevitable. Once this hook is set, the user will begin to feel uncomfortable within a few hours of the last dose. If no drug is forthcoming, by twenty-four to forty-eight hours life becomes a miserable mix of sweats, cramps, shaking, nausea, vomiting, and diarrhea. For most users, these symptoms subside within a week, and as rotten as they may feel, an adult in reasonable health will survive this ordeal even without any medical support. (This may not be the case, however, for the unborn child of a pregnant woman undergoing withdrawal.) Unfortunately, a user may crave this drug and stumble back into its enslaving grip months after withdrawal symptoms have completely disappeared.

What are the stages of drug abuse?

Experts in adolescent substance-abuse problems have identified a common progression of alcohol- and drug-related behaviors that move from bad to worse. Though it is not a foregone conclusion that everyone who experiments with drugs will progress to the worst stages of involvement, a child can already have incurred a lot of damage before parents or others notice that something is wrong. Secretive adolescent behavior and skillful lying, combined with parental denial ("No one in our family could have a drug problem!"), may delay identification of the problem. While paranoia and daily inquisitions around the breakfast table are counterproductive, wise parents will keep their eyes and ears open and promptly take action if they see any signs that a problem may be developing.

Stage one: Experimentation—entering the drug gateway
Characteristics:
- Use is occasional, sporadic, often unplanned—weekends, summer nights, someone's unsupervised party.
- Use is precipitated by peer pressure, curiosity, thrill seeking, a desire to look and feel grown-up.

- Gateway drugs are usually used—cigarettes, alcohol, marijuana, possibly inhalants.
- A drug high is easier to experience because tolerance has not developed.

You may notice:
- Tobacco or alcohol on the breath or intoxicated behavior.
- Little change in normal behavior between episodes of drug use.

Stage two: More regular drug use—leaving the land of the living
Characteristics:
- Alcohol and other drugs are used not only on weekends but also on weekdays, not only with friends but when alone.
- Quantities of alcohol and drugs increase as tolerance develops; hangovers become more common.
- Blackouts may occur—periods of time in which drugs or alcohol prevent normal memories from forming. "What happened last night?" becomes a frequent question.
- More time and attention are focused on when the next drug experience will occur.
- Fellow drinkers or drug users become preferred companions.

You may notice:
- Your teen will be out of the house later at night, overnight, or all weekend.
- School performance worsens—unexplained school absences.
- Outside activities such as sports are dropped.
- Decreased contact with friends who don't use drugs.
- Disappearance of money or other valuables.

- Child withdraws from the family, is increasingly sullen and hostile.
- User is caught in one or many lies.

Stage three: Waist-deep in the mire of addiction—and sinking
Characteristics:
- Alcohol and drugs become the primary focus of attention.
- Becoming high is a daily event.
- There is a use of harder, more dangerous drugs.
- More money is spent each week on drugs; theft or dealing may become part of drug-seeking behavior.
- Adolescent displays increasing social isolation; no contact with non-drug-using friends; more drug use in isolation rather than socially.

You may notice the behaviors listed above, plus:
- Escalation of conflicts at home.
- Loss of nearly all control of the adolescent.
- Possible discovery of a stash of drugs at home.
- Arrest(s) for possession of drugs or dealing them, or for driving under the influence.

Stage four: Drowning in addiction
Characteristics:
- Constant state of intoxication; being high is routine, even at school or job (if they attend at all).
- Blackouts increase in frequency.
- Physical appearance deteriorates—weight loss, infections, poor self-care.
- Injectable drugs are possibly used.
- Involvement in casual sexual relationships (at times in exchange for drugs).

- User will likely be involved with theft, dealing, and other criminal activity.
- Guilt, self-hatred, and thoughts of suicide increase.
- Any apparent interest in spiritual matters is abandoned.

You are likely to be dealing with:
- Complete loss of control over adolescent's behavior; escalation of conflict, possibly to the point of violence.
- Ongoing denial by user that drugs are a problem.
- Increasing problems with the law and time spent with police, attorneys, hearings, court officials, etc.
- Negative effects on other siblings because the family is preoccupied or overwhelmed by consequences of drug user's behavior.

This descent into drug hell is a nightmare that no parent envisions while rocking a newborn baby or escorting an eager five-year-old to kindergarten. But it can happen in any neighborhood, church, or family, even in those in which parents have provided a stable and loving home environment. In fact, it is often in such homes that a drug problem goes undetected until it has reached an advanced and dangerous stage. "This can't be happening, not in my house!" But if it does, parental guilt, anger, and depression can undermine the responses necessary to restore order.

How can I help my teenager avoid drug abuse?
Drug abuse is so widespread in our culture that you cannot expect to isolate your teenager from exposure to it. However, as with diseases caused by bacteria and viruses, you can institute infection-control measures. Specifically, take steps to reduce the likelihood of contact with drugs and build your teen's immunity to using them. These measures should be ongoing, deliberate, and proactive.

Model behavior you want your children to follow. When it comes to drugs, two adages are worth noting: "Children learn what they live" and "What parents allow in moderation their children will do in excess." Though not absolute truths, these maxims reflect the reality that kids are looking to their parents for cues as to what is acceptable behavior, while at the same time developing the discernment required to understand what moderation is all about.

If you smoke, your offspring will probably do likewise. But it's never too late to quit, and your decision to give up cigarettes will make an important statement to all the members of your family—especially if you are willing to hold yourself accountable to them.

If you consume alcohol at home, what role does it play in your life? Does it flow freely on a daily basis? Do you need a drink to unwind at the end of the day? Is it a necessary ingredient at every party or family get-together? If so, your children will get the picture that alcohol is a painkiller, tension reliever, and the life of the party, and they will likely use it in a similar fashion. For their sake (and yours), take whatever steps are necessary to live without alcohol. Many parents decide to abstain while rearing their children in order to send an unambiguous message to steer clear of it. Others feel that modeling modest use of alcohol without intoxication (while speaking clearly against underage drinking, drunkenness, driving under the influence, and other irresponsible behaviors) equips children and teenagers to make sensible decisions later in life.

What about your medicine cabinet? If you are stressed, upset, or uncomfortable, are drugs the way you usually spell *r-e-l-i-e-f*? Have you accumulated a collection of prescription medications that you appear to utilize freely when the going gets tough? Kids aren't blind. If they see the adults around them frequently taking "legitimate" drugs to dull their pain, why can't they use their own drugs of choice to do the same?

Even when medications have been prescribed appropriately, overuse and even addiction is possible with certain types of drugs. If you have a chronic condition for which habit-forming medications have been prescribed, you would be wise not only to model responsible use but also to demonstrate when possible your commitment to find other types of treatment (for example, physical therapy, exercise, or counseling) that might be appropriate. Note: The appropriate use of antidepressants to treat the biochemistry of mood disorders does *not* represent a potential abuse situation. These medications are neither addicting nor habit-forming and are not sold on the street to create an artificial drug high.

Finally, if you use marijuana and other street drugs, whether for recreational purposes or because of an addiction problem, you are putting the parental stamp of approval not only on the drugs but also on breaking the law. For your own and your family's sake, seek help immediately and bring this dangerous behavior to an end.

Build identity and attitudes that are resistant to drug use. This is an ongoing project, beginning during the first years of your child's life. Specifically:

- Create an environment that consistently balances love and limits. Teenagers who know they are loved unconditionally are less likely to seek "pain relief" through drugs, and those who have learned to live within appropriate boundaries will have better impulse control and self-discipline.
- Instill respect and awe for the God-given gift of a body and mind—even one that isn't perfect.
- Help your teenager become a student of consequences—not only in connection with drugs but with other behaviors as well. Talk about good and bad choices and the logic behind them. "Just say no" is an appropriate motto for kids

to learn, but understanding *why* it is wrong to use harmful substances will build more solid resistance.

- Build a positive sense of identity with your family. This means not only openly affirming and appreciating each member, but also putting forth the time and effort for meaningful and fun shared experiences. A strong sense of belonging to a loving family builds accountability ("Our family doesn't use drugs") and helps prevent loneliness, which can be a setup for a drug experience.

- Encourage church-related activities (including family devotions) that build a meaningful, personal faith. Reliance on God should be the cornerstone of drug-treatment programs, and it makes no sense to leave the spiritual dimension out of the prevention process. A vibrant faith reinforces the concept that the future is worth protecting, stabilizes the emotions during turbulent years, and provides a healthy response to the aches and pains of life. In addition, an awareness of God's presence and a desire not to dishonor Him can be strong deterrents to destructive behavior.

Begin talking early about smoking, alcohol, and drugs. Because experimentation with drugs and alcohol commonly begins during the grade-school years, start appropriate countermeasures in very young children. A five-year-old may not be ready for a lecture about the physiology of cocaine addiction, but you should be ready to offer commentary when you and your child see someone smoking or drinking, whether in real life or in a movie or TV program. If intoxication is portrayed as humorous, don't be shy about setting the record straight.

Keep talking about smoking, alcohol, and drugs as opportunities arise. Make an effort to stay one step ahead of your adolescent's knowledge of the drug scene. If you hear about an athlete, rock star, or celebrity who uses drugs, be certain that everyone in the family understands that no amount of fame or fortune excuses this behavior. If a famous person is dealing with the consequences of drug use (such as being dropped from a team or suffering medical or legal consequences), make sure your kids hear the cautionary tale. If you become aware of a person (whether a celebrity or not) who is taking positive steps to deal with a drug or alcohol problem, be sure to acknowledge and praise that effort.

Be aware of current trends in your community, and look for local meetings or lectures where abuse problems are being discussed. Find out what's going on—not only from the experts but from your kids and their friends. If you hear that someone is smoking, drinking, inhaling, or injecting drugs, talk about it. What are they using? What consequences are likely? Why is it wrong? What help do they need?

All this assumes you are available to have these conversations. Be careful, because the time when you may be the busiest with career or other responsibilities may also be the time when your teenager at home most needs your input. If you're too overworked, overcommitted, and overtired to keep tabs on the home front, you may wake up one day to find a major drug problem on your doorstep.

Don't allow your teenager to go to a party, sleepover, or other activity that isn't supervised by someone you trust. Don't blindly assume that the presence of a grown-up guarantees a safe environment. Get to know your kid's friends' parents, not just your kid's friends. Make certain your teenager knows you will pick him up anytime, anywhere—no questions asked—if he finds himself in a situation where alcohol or drugs are being used. And be sure to praise him for a wise and mature decision if he calls.

Have the courage to curtail your teenager's contact with drug users. The epidemic of drug abuse spreads person to person. Whether a recent acquaintance or a long-term bosom buddy, if one (or more) of your teenager's friends is known to be actively using alcohol or drugs, you must impose restrictions on the relationship. You might, for example, stipulate that your adolescent can spend time with that person only in your home—without any closed doors and when you are around. However, even with these limits in place, you will need to keep track of who is influencing whom.

Create significant consequences to discourage alcohol and drug use. Teenagers may not be scared by facts, figures, and gory details. Even the most ominous warnings may not override their belief in their own immortality, especially when other compelling emotions such as the need for peer acceptance are operating at full throttle.

You may improve the odds by making it clear that you consider the use of cigarettes, alcohol, or illegal drugs a very serious matter. Judgment regarding punishments fitting crimes will be necessary, of course. Loss of driving, dating, or even cell phone privileges for an extended period of time may be in order.

What do I do if a problem has already developed?

Even in families that are close-knit, hold strong values, and practice ongoing drug proofing, there are no guarantees that substance abuse won't affect your children. The problems may range from a brief encounter with cigarettes to an episode of intoxication (perhaps with legal consequences) or may even involve addiction. As you begin to cope with the chemical intruder(s) in your home, keep the following principles in mind:

Don't deny or ignore the problem. If you do, it is likely to continue to worsen until your family life is turned inside out. Take the bull by the horns—but be sure to find out exactly how big and ugly the bull is. The marijuana cigarette you discovered may be a onetime experiment—or the tip of an iceberg. Talk to your teenager about it—but also talk to siblings, friends, and anyone else who knows what she's up to. You may not like what you hear, but it's better to get the hard truth now than a ghastly surprise later.

Don't wallow in false guilt. Most parents assume a great deal of self-blame when a drug problem erupts in their home. If you carry some responsibility for what has happened (whether you know about it immediately or find out later on), face up to it, confess it to God and your family, and then get on with the task of helping your child. But remember that your teenager must deal with his own responsibility as well.

Seek help from people experienced with treating drug problems. Talk to your physician and pastor. They should be part of your team, even if in a supporting role. It is likely that you will receive a referral to a professional who is experienced in organizing a family intervention. This may include educational sessions, individual and family counseling, medical treatment, and long-term follow-up. When the user's behavior is out of control and she is unwilling to acknowledge the problem, a carefully planned confrontation by family members and others affected may need to be carried out under the supervision of an experienced counselor. The goal is to convince the drug user in a firm but loving way of the need for change—*now*. The confrontation should include specific alternatives for the type of treatment she will undergo and a clear-cut "or else . . ." if she is not willing to cooperate.

Be prepared to make difficult, "tough love" decisions. If you have a drug-dependent adolescent who will not submit to treatment and insists on continuing drug use and other destructive actions, you will need to take the stomach-churning step of informing him that he cannot continue to live in your home while carrying on this behavior. This will be necessary not only to motivate him to change, but also to prevent his drug-induced turbulence from destroying the rest of your family.

If you must take this drastic step, it would be helpful to present him with one or more options. These might include entering an inpatient drug-treatment center, halfway house, boot-camp program, or youth home, or staying with a relative or another family who is willing to accept him for a defined period of time. More ominous possibilities may need to be discussed as well, such as making him a ward of the court or even turning him over to the police if he has been involved in criminal activity. If you continue to shield him from the consequences of his behavior or bail him out when his drugs get him into trouble, he will not change, and you will be left with deep-seated anger and frustration.

Don't look for or expect quick-fix solutions. It is normal to wish for a single intervention that will make a drug problem go away. But one conversation, counseling session, prayer time, or trip to the doctor won't be enough. Think in terms of a comprehensive response encompassing specific treatment and counseling and the gamut of your child's life—home, school, friends, and church.

Remember the father of the Prodigal Son. "Tough love" means allowing the consequences of bad decisions to be fully experienced by the one who is making them. It also means your teenager must know that your love for her is so deep and secure it will never die. Never give up hope, never stop praying, and never slam the door on reconciliation and restoration when your child comes to her senses.

CHAPTER 6

THWARTING THREATS TO A TEEN'S SELF-CONCEPT

Scorn has broken my heart
and has left me helpless;
I looked for sympathy, but there was none,
for comforters, but I found none.

PSALM 69:20

IN CHAPTER 2, we described the important task of developing a stable, healthy identity during the teen years. There are more than a few potential obstacles to that process, and we have just considered two of them—sexual activity and drug use—in chapters 4 and 5. In this chapter, we will look at three more tough topics that can batter or even derail a teen's self-concept: bullying (which affects almost every child or adolescent at some time in life), eating disorders, and depression, which are less common but still very serious issues.

What is bullying?

Bullying involves ongoing aggressive behavior intended to cause harm or distress in a relationship where there is an imbalance of power, physical or otherwise. Bullying can occur at any stage of life, but it is particularly common—and destructive—during childhood and adolescence. Sadly, but not surprisingly, the targets of bullying are often those who are poorly equipped to deal with it: the small, the weak, those who look or act a little different from the crowd, and those who have difficulty making and keeping friends. Bullying goes well beyond the usual horseplay, verbal and otherwise, of childhood and adolescence. It is essentially child abuse perpetrated by peers, and it may take a variety of forms:

- *Verbal*. Insults, name-calling, racial or ethnic slurs. Verbal bullying is the most common type, affecting boys and girls equally.
- *Physical*. Hitting, kicking, shoving, or other direct bodily injury, as well as destruction of property. Boys are more likely to be physically bullied by other boys.
- *Social*. Spreading gossip and rumors (often sexually related), exclusion, or outright isolation. These are more common forms of bullying among girls.
- *Electronic*. "Cyberbullying" on the Internet or through text messaging on cell phones.[18]

Bullying is not restricted to any particular geographic location, community setting (urban, suburban, or rural), ethnic group, or socioeconomic status. It can happen anywhere. It is more common at school—in the classroom, hallway, playground, or lunchroom—than on the way to or from school.

The 2009 National Youth Risk Behavior Survey found that 20 percent of high school students had been bullied at school during the previous twelve months, and 5 percent avoided going to school at least one day during the previous month because of concerns over safety.[19] Unfortunately, statistics only dimly reflect the pain endured by victims of bullying. Aside from any physical injuries they might sustain, victims are also more likely to suffer from anxiety, depression, and physical complaints such as head-aches, abdominal pain, and fatigue.

Reluctance to go to school (or wherever the bullying occurs) is a common manifestation and may result in numerous absences. *When a child or adolescent experiences frequent school absences, especially due to physical complaints for which a medical evaluation reveals no specific cause, victimization by bullying should be considered as a possible—or likely—cause.* Unfortunately, children or teenagers all too often are reluctant to report what has happened to parents or school officials—even if asked directly—because of a conviction that nothing can be done about it, lack of confidence that teachers or administrators will take effective action, and (most important) fear of retaliation.

Even more worrisome is the connection between bullying and violence, by both the perpetrator and the victim. Teens who bully are more likely to be involved or injured in fights, and to steal, vandalize, smoke, use alcohol, drop out of school, and carry a weapon. Furthermore, teens who have been repeatedly victimized may decide to seek spectacular and tragic revenge.

What are some measures I can take to prevent bullying?

Parents have the primary responsibility for training, instilling, and modeling values in their children, including respect for other people, regardless of age, appearance, or other characteristics. Bullying, at its core, is an expression of disrespect. Thus the atmosphere at home should be one in which abusive speech or actions, whether directed at others within or outside of the family, are clearly understood to be unacceptable for everyone—children and adults alike.

More specifically, you can impress on your children that they are not to participate in bullying, whether as individuals or in a group, and that they should report bullying to an adult (teacher, administrator, or parent), whether they themselves or someone

else is the target. Furthermore, when possible, they should understand that coming to the assistance of someone who is being bullied is not only appropriate, but an act of courage.

What should I do if my child is being bullied?

Be aware of the following indicators that may suggest a child is
being harassed:

- Injuries—unexplained bruises, cuts, or scratches
- Torn, damaged, or missing clothing or other belongings
- Anxiety, tearfulness, moodiness, and resistance to going
  to school
- Ongoing physical symptoms—especially headaches,
  stomachaches, or fatigue—that are invoked as a reason
  to stay home

If you are suspicious, ask questions that express your interest
and concern: "How are things going at school? Is anything—or
anyone—giving you a hard time?" Your child may be reluctant to
reveal what has happened, and you may need to exercise some
persistence to find out. If bullying has indeed occurred, make sure
your teenager understands that you take it very seriously, that you
intend to take appropriate action, and that keeping silent will only
allow the bullying to continue. You will need to get as much information as possible: who, when, where, and what happened. If
there have been witnesses to the bullying, gather information from
them as well.

Assuming the bullying has happened at school, make an
appointment as soon as possible with the principal or the administrator designated to handle this type of problem. Most likely this
person will be ready and willing to put the heat on anyone who is
involved in bullying, but he will need specifics. Tell the story, but
also provide information in writing, and be sure to take note of

the response to your concern. You may want to arrange a meeting with the perpetrator and one or both parents in a school official's office. Your posture should be calm, but resolute: Look the bully in the eye and make it abundantly clear that even one further episode will bring disastrous consequences and that you expect the parents to cooperate.

If the harassment continues and the principal or parents of the perpetrator appear unwilling to take appropriate action, they should be put on notice that the problem may be taken to a higher level of school administration, an attorney, the police, or all of the above. If the problem involves risks of extreme violence or gang activity, you will need to seek advice from law-enforcement personnel. In a worst-case scenario, a change of school (or homeschooling) may be necessary to bring your adolescent through this situation in one piece. *Do whatever it takes (within the bounds of the law) to protect your child's safety and self-respect.*

What if my child is the bully?

Whatever you do, don't shrug it off or deny the problem. Get the facts. You should get your child's side of the story, but also diligently seek input both from school officials and from anyone else who was involved, including the victim(s) of the bullying. If the evidence (or your teen's own admission) points to her involvement in bullying, you must make it clear that not only is this behavior unacceptable, but it will not be tolerated. If continued, it will lead to serious consequences imposed by you, the school, and possibly the law.

You will need to contact the parents of the victim(s) to apologize and express your determination to prevent further episodes. As a gesture of integrity and courage, you might want to arrange a meeting with the other family at an appropriate location so that a formal apology can be made by your child, as well as an offer of restitution for any expenses (involving medical care or property damage) related to the incident(s).

If others have been involved in bullying—perpetrators often act in groups—you should take the lead in contacting their parents to encourage corrective and restorative action.

If your teenager has been involved in multiple bullying incidents, you should arrange for him to undergo counseling, both for evaluation and prevention of further episodes. Other issues—depression, drug use, impulse control, and even prior victimization (since some bullies have been bullied themselves)—may need to be addressed. *This is a family issue*, so be prepared to participate in some important discussions in the counselor's office.

Suggested resources you might find useful include the following:

- *Help! My Child Is Being Bullied* by Bill Maier (Focus on the Family, 2006).
- The Stop Bullying Now website (www.stopbullying.gov) offers numerous resources for kids, parents, and educators.
- The STRYVE (Striving to Reduce Youth Violence Everywhere) website of the Centers for Disease Control and Prevention (www.safeyouth.gov) has information on a broad range of topics related to violence committed by and against the young.

How do eating disorders affect teens?

Though excessive body fat is a continuing physical and emotional problem for millions of teenagers,[20] powerful cultural forces provoke behaviors that pose even more serious threats to the young. We are saturated night and day with images of beautiful, shapely, impossibly sleek women or buff, tight-muscled men. This leads many, especially prepubertal and adolescent girls, into dangerous thinking: *If only I could look like that, my problems would be over.*

Often this fantasy fuels a deeply felt desire for physical perfection that collides rudely with the imperfect appearance of the very real bodies they see in the mirror.

This conflict can lead not only to erratic eating habits and dieting, which are not without some risks, but also to the more severely disordered eating patterns known as *bulimia* and *anorexia nervosa*. These eating disorders arise from a complex interaction of anxiety, depression, life issues, and concern over body image that converge into compulsive and often highly dangerous behaviors.

Because eating disorders are not routinely reported by physicians and counselors to government or professional associations, estimates of the number of people affected vary widely. Of those afflicted, 90 percent are women, and most are between the ages of twelve and thirty-five. Athletes, models, dancers, and others in the entertainment industry are at particular risk, usually because of intense concern about maintaining a particular, often unrealistic, appearance or level of performance.

What factors contribute to a teen developing an eating disorder?

Though each case is unique, potential contributing factors include the following:

Personality and psychological factors. A typical profile of an anorexia patient is a perfectionistic, high-achieving, adolescent female. She may be seen as a compliant, "good" girl by her parents (one or both of whom might also be perfectionists), and she usually does not rebel or have much of a social or dating life. While excelling in many areas, she may berate herself over any performance that falls short of perfection. Some researchers theorize that refusing to eat may serve as a form of rebellion or that it may represent one area of her life over which she can exercise total control. Bulimics, on the other hand, are less predictable in personality and attributes, although alcohol or drug abuse may be a concurrent issue. In nearly all individuals with either type of eating disorder, anxiety and depression play a significant role.

Biochemical factors. Chemical messengers in the brain called neurotransmitters are known to be associated with mood, emotional stability, appetite, and sleep. Many people are genetically vulnerable to changes in neurotransmitter levels, which can lead to overt depression and anxiety disorders, as well as a condition called obsessive-compulsive disorder (OCD)—performing certain repetitive acts or ritualistic behavior to relieve anxiety. Neurotransmitter imbalances appear to play a role in the origin of eating disorders, and many features of anorexia bear a striking resemblance to those of OCD.

Cultural factors. In developed countries, advertisements, films, videos, and TV programs continually display images of bodily perfection, especially for females. Those who are shapely, sleek—and most of all, *thin*—are seen as successful, sophisticated, desirable, and apparently free of emotional or personal pain. A vulnerable individual who desperately desires these attributes but cannot attain them through normal means may engage in unhealthy and extreme behaviors.

The "pro-ana"/"pro-mia" subculture. Some people with eating disorders (especially teens) have been known to share "tricks of the trade" with one another. But a more disturbing development over the past several years has been the emergence of websites proclaiming anorexia and bulimia to be positive lifestyles and not disorders. Posting "Thin Commandments" (such as "being thin is more important than being healthy" and "being thin and not eating are signs of true willpower and success"), bingeing and purging tips, and "thinspiration" stories, these sites offer an unsettling look into the mind-set of those who are not interested in "recovering" from their ongoing behavior.

What is anorexia?

Anorexia nervosa is a condition of self-imposed starvation that eventually leads to a body weight at least 15 percent below the expected level for an individual's age and height. Affecting as many as one in one hundred girls and young women, it is characterized by an extreme fear of—or antagonism toward—gaining weight and a striking disturbance of body image: The anorexic who appears grossly emaciated will look in the mirror and see herself as overweight. This distorted perception typically is stubbornly resistant to feedback from families, friends, and health professionals, even in the face of serious physical and medical consequences.

As more weight is lost, the fear of gaining weight intensifies rather than diminishes, leading to nonstop preoccupation with eating and weight. Behaviors seen in obsessive-compulsive disorder often attend anorexia as well. What little food is eaten will usually be derived only from "safe" low-calorie sources, often measured out in precise quantities and then consumed in an exacting, almost ritualistic manner. Food might be cut into tiny pieces and then arranged and rearranged on the plate to give the impression that some of it has been eaten. Anorexics may obsess over the number of calories they consume from medication or even from licking a postage stamp. Often they carefully monitor body measurements such as upper arm circumference. The fervor with which calories are restricted is frequently applied to burning them as well, and an anorexic individual will sometimes exercise vigorously for hours every day.

Why is anorexia a danger to health?

It should come as no surprise that medical consequences, most arising from the body's attempt to conserve energy, become more serious as starvation and weight loss continue. With loss of fat and circulating estrogen, the intricate hormonal interplay of a woman's monthly cycle shuts down, a condition called amenorrhea. (The absence of three consecutive menstrual periods is one of the diagnostic criteria for anorexia nervosa.) This, combined with an ongoing inadequate intake of nutrients and calcium, leads to loss of bone density, which can cause stress fractures, especially during intense exercise.

Starvation leads to reduced capacity of the stomach, delays in its emptying of food, and constipation, all of which may be falsely interpreted by the anorexic as weight gain. Dry skin, thinning of the scalp hair, and development of a fine hair growth on the body, called *lanugo*, typically occur. Loss of fat stores and metabolic energy conservation lead to a lower body temperature, often causing the anorexic individual to wear more layers of clothing to keep warm. (Wearing extra clothing may also be a strategy to hide changes in body weight during medical checkups.) More serious complications arise in the heart, which typically slows its contraction rate and decreases in size in response to efforts to conserve energy. Heart rhythm might become irregular, sometimes to a degree that is life threatening, especially in the presence of purging behavior that can deplete the body of potassium.

For all these reasons, anorexia nervosa should be considered a very serious condition with lethal risks. At least 5 percent—some sources say as high as 20 percent—of anorexics die from starvation, cardiac arrest, or suicide, giving this disorder the dubious distinction of having one of the highest death rates of any mental-health condition. (The worst death rates are observed among those with a long duration of anorexia, more severe weight loss, poor family support, and multiple relapses despite treatment.)

What is bulimia?

Bulimia nervosa is characterized by behavior known as bingeing and purging, which may continue for decades. During a binge, an individual quickly consumes an enormous amount of food containing many thousands of calories, often hardly even chewing or tasting it. The resulting physical and emotional discomfort will then provoke a purge, usually involving self-induced vomiting. Bulimics often use diuretics (medications that increase urine output) and laxatives, sometimes in dangerous quantities, in a misguided belief that the medication will somehow help rid the body of food that isn't lost through vomiting. Bingeing and purging cycles may occur a few times a week or, in severe cases, several times daily.

Bulimia is more common than anorexia, affecting an estimated one to 3 percent of women in Western countries at some time in life, but it frequently goes undetected because most episodes take place in secret and typically do not lead to significant weight loss. (However, some individuals with anorexia may engage in binge-and-purge behaviors.) Nevertheless, bulimia can have many serious medical consequences.

How can bulimia endanger a teen's health?

The repeated exposure of teeth to stomach acid (during vomiting) erodes enamel, causes a yellowish discoloration, and sometimes leads to decay. The throat and esophagus may become chronically inflamed, and the salivary glands—especially the parotid glands that lie directly in front of the ears—can become enlarged in response to continuing episodes of vomiting. Repeated use of laxatives often leads to severe constipation, and heavy diuretic use may adversely affect kidney function.

Potentially dangerous disturbances in heart rhythm can arise from the repeated loss of potassium from vomiting, as well as from excessive ingestion of diuretics and laxatives. Other equally serious (but fortunately uncommon) events include bleeding—and even rupture—of the esophagus or stomach from frequent vomiting. Food aspirated into the trachea during vomiting can cause choking or pneumonia.

More recently, the concept of *binge-eating disorder*, which some experts consider a form of bulimia (but others characterize as an obesity disorder), has received increasing attention among those who study eating disorders. There is not a consensus at this time as to a precise definition, or whether binge eating should even be formally classified as a behavior disorder, but some believe it is the *most common* eating disorder.

Binge-eating disorder involves repeated episodes (lasting at least two hours) of eating excessive amounts of food, but without the purging and exercising behaviors seen with bulimia. Binge eaters often eat alone, consume their food quickly until they experience discomfort or pain, and are aware that their eating is out of control. Depression, anxiety, and frequent unsuccessful dieting attempts are common. Because binge eaters don't vomit or use diuretics or laxatives to counter their excessive food intake, they are not prone to the medical complications of bulimia. Not surprisingly, most (though not all) binge eaters are overweight. However, the converse is not true: Most overweight people are not binge eaters.

If my child has an eating disorder, what are some treatment options?

Because eating disorders can put one's health or life in serious jeopardy, they should be taken very seriously. Initiating treatment can be difficult for bulimics, who hide so much of their disordered behavior, and for anorexics, who may stubbornly deny that they need help and undermine (or vigorously oppose) therapeutic efforts.

In order to be effective, treatment must address a variety of issues and will often require a team approach. A thorough medical evaluation is vitally important and will sometimes reveal a variety of problems that need attention. Counseling will be needed on a long-term basis and should involve the entire family. Antidepressant medication that normalizes neurotransmitter levels can help stabilize mood, relieve depression, and reduce the obsessive component of anorexia. A dietitian should also be consulted to provide nutritional input and accountability. Pastoral counseling (ideally by someone who has some familiarity with eating disorders) can help address issues of guilt and shame, as well as critical worldview and spiritual issues, especially for those who see their eating behavior as a means of achieving self-mastery and perfection. In severe cases of anorexia, hospitalization and medically supervised feeding may be necessary to prevent a fatal outcome.

How can I prevent my child from developing an eating disorder?

It is impossible to predict who might develop an eating disorder, but it is possible for parents to reduce an adolescent's risk in the following ways:

- Beware of perfectionism, especially in regard to your teenager's weight or physical appearance. Your child must understand that her worth and your acceptance of her are unconditional, not based on physical beauty or perfect performance.
- Beware of demands on an adolescent to "make weight" for an athletic team, slim down for a cheerleading or dance team, or subject his or her body to stringent dietary restrictions for any reason.
- Help your teenager understand that body shape and build have a strong genetic basis and that few women are capable of attaining cover-girl status, even with intense effort.

- Eliminate from your own and your family's conversations jokes or other demeaning comments about the appearance of others.
- Point out to your children how advertising and other media put forth images of beauty and body image that are out of reach for nearly everyone.
- Be a good role model in your own eating and exercise habits, and be careful about openly criticizing your own body appearance.
- Focus on relationships and building emotional intimacy in your family, rather than on food-related issues. Be aware of the purposes that food might be serving in your home, beyond relieving hunger. Is it used for comfort or reward? Is it used to relieve boredom? Be careful not to use food as a substitute for hugs or for saying, "I love you."

What is depression?

Depression is by far the most common and important emotional health problem in America. In our culture, the term *depression* is applied to a broad spectrum of situations in which a person feels unhappy. Here, however, we are dealing specifically with what is called clinical or major depression—not a temporary emotional slump, such as after watching a sad movie or receiving a traffic ticket or even after a day in which one thing after another goes sour.

All of the difficulties and heartaches arising from depression apply not only to adults but also to children and teens, often with greater intensity. What is more disturbing is that depression kills the young more frequently than it does adults. The rate of suicide among the young is heartbreaking: It is the fourth leading cause of death in children between the ages of ten and fourteen, third among those between the ages of fifteen and nineteen, and second among college-age men and women. Every year in the United

States, suicide ends nearly five thousand lives between the ages of fifteen and twenty-four, and the rate of suicide in this age group has increased nearly threefold since 1960.[21] The number may actually be higher, because many accidents (such as drug overdoses, drownings, or fatal automobile crashes involving a lone teenage driver) may in fact be suicides.

Clinical depression involves a *persistent* (lasting two weeks or longer) and usually *disruptive* disturbance of mood, and often affects other bodily functions as well. As we list the common characteristics of depression, it is important to note that these may manifest themselves quite differently in children and teenagers compared with adults. In fact, because the behaviors provoked by depression are frequently confused with the normal emotional and physical upheavals of growing up, at one time it was erroneously assumed that this condition occurred rarely, if at all, before adulthood. In each symptom category, we will mention some of the unique variations seen in young people who are depressed.

Persistent sadness and/or irritability. Most parents complain at some point, if not frequently, that their teenager has a "lousy attitude." As described in chapter 2, it isn't at all unusual for teens to experience emotions and mood swings that seem out of proportion to the circumstances. But the depressed child or teenager seems to be in a perpetual slump.

Unfortunately, you won't hear a young person say, "In case you haven't noticed, I've been depressed for the past several weeks." Instead, you may see one—or more likely several—of the following distress signals that might appear disconnected:

- Continued overt sadness or moping; frequent episodes of crying.
- A loss of enthusiasm or interest in things that were once favorite activities.

- Increasing withdrawal and isolation from family and friends.
- Poor school performance: plummeting grades, loss of interest in schoolwork, and frequent absences.
- Outbursts of anger, arguing, disrespectful comments, or blatant hostility toward everyone at home.
- Repeated complaints about being bored or tired.
- Overt acting out: drug or alcohol use, running away, sexual activity, fighting, vandalism, or other antisocial activity.

This does not mean, of course, that all negative attitudes and actions are manifestations of depression. In chapter 2, we offered a number of suggestions for dealing with the emotional climate of adolescence, and you may want to review that material if you are encountering turbulence. But if you are confronted with persistent disturbances in emotions and behavior, consider the possibility of depression, and more importantly, seek input from a qualified counselor, physician, or both.

Painful thoughts. If we compare depression to a very long, sad song, the mood disturbance just described is the mournful or agitated music. But accompanying the unhappy melody are painful lyrics—words that express, over and over again, a view of life that is anything but upbeat.

People who have experienced both depression and bodily injuries (for example, a major fracture) usually will confirm that physical pain is easier to manage than emotional pain. Usually, one can expect physical pain to resolve or at least become tolerable. But no such hopeful expectations accompany painful thoughts, which can roll into the mind like waves from an ocean that extends to a limitless, bleak horizon.

Painful thoughts, like a disturbed mood, can have several manifestations:

- *Relentless introspection.* Teenagers tend to be highly self-conscious during the normal (and necessary) process of establishing their identity during the transition into adulthood. But depression magnifies and warps this natural introspection into a mental inquisition. The inward gaze not only becomes a relentless stare, but it focuses exclusively on shortcomings. It can also move into some dangerous territory: "Wouldn't I and everyone else be better off if I weren't here? Why does it matter at this point whether I live or die?"

- *Negative self-concept.* Physical appearance, intelligence, competence, acceptance, and general worth are all subject to relentless and exaggerated criticism. This is not a healthy examination of areas that need improvement, nor repentance for wrongdoing that might lead to improvements in attitude and behavior. Instead, unrealistic self-reproach for whatever isn't going well in life—or at the opposite extreme, spreading blame to everyone else—is likely to dominate a depressed child's or adolescent's thoughts and interfere with positive changes.

A depressed teenager slumps into a lunchroom chair and moans, "I'm fat. I'm never gonna get a date. I'm stupid. I'll never pass calculus. I feel miserable. I'm never going to feel good again." Her friends, if they bother to hang around to listen to this litany of woe, may argue with her. "You're not stupid. Stop talking that way." If she persists in her lament, they may become fed up and agree with her, if only to end her complaints: "Okay, so you're fat and stupid. C'mon, we're gonna be late for class." Her parents might unwittingly make a similar mistake in trying to bolster her spirits: "What are you talking about? You look fine to us, and you're smart. Enough of this negative talk!" Such responses only build feelings of rejection and a conviction that "no one understands me."

This state of affairs will be drastically worsened for those who have been subjected to emotional, physical, or sexual abuse during childhood or adolescence. Whether these assaults attack the heart ("You're so stupid!" "Why can't you be like _____?") or the body, they create a sense of worthlessness that supplies powerful fuel for an ongoing depression.

- *Anxiety.* Persistent worry, whether focused on a specific issue or a free-floating apprehension that encompasses most daily activities, frequently accompanies depression. Though a modest level of concern is not only normal but necessary to motivate appropriate precautions for everyday activities, the anxiety associated with depression is disabling and actually interferes with effective responses to life's challenges.

- *Hopelessness.* This is particularly troublesome for teenagers, not only because they may feel emotions so strongly, but also because they haven't lived long enough to understand the ebb and flow of life's problems and pleasures. Most adults facing a crisis will think back to the last twenty-seven crises they have already lived through and will have gained enough perspective to know that this current trial will probably pass as well. But when young people collide with a crisis (or at least what appears to be one from their perspective), they usually have far fewer experiences with which to compare it and a limited fund of responses. If they can't see a satisfactory route past the current problem, it is no wonder they might begin to think that their life "is over" or "not worth living." This dark view of life isn't helped by some powerful voices in popular culture (especially in music) that focus on rage, alienation, despair, and death.

What are the physical symptoms of depression?

Physiological responses in the body routinely accompany emotional events, and so it should come as little surprise that physical symptoms are often associated with depression. Common problems include the following:

- *Insomnia and other sleep disturbances.* Difficulty falling asleep at night, awakening too early in the morning, and fitful sleep in between are very common in depressed individuals. This may be accompanied by a desire to sleep during the day. Some people experience *hypersomnia* (sleeping for excessively long periods of time), in which sleep seems to serve as an escape from the misery of waking hours. An important sign that depression is improving is the normalization of sleeping patterns.

- *Appetite changes.* Loss of appetite and weight or nonstop hunger and weight gain are common during depression. Such changes can complicate a teenager's normal concerns about appearance.

- *Physiological problems.* Depressed individuals often have a variety of physical complaints. Fatigue is almost universally present. Headaches, dizziness, nausea, abdominal cramps, episodes of shortness of breath, and heart palpitations are not at all unusual. Sometimes poor concentration, unusual pain patterns, or altered sensations in various parts of the body will raise concerns about a serious medical disorder. Very often, an evaluation for an assortment of symptoms will uncover no evidence of an underlying disease, but will lead an attentive physician to suspect depression. The absence of a serious diagnosis may bring a sigh of relief to a young patient (and most certainly to his parents) but can also cause dismay. "Are you saying all of this is in my [my child's] head?" is a typical response. In fact, the symptoms are very real and a predictable component of depression. When depression improves with treatment, so do the physical symptoms.

Why do teens become depressed?

A complex blend of genetic, biochemical, personal, family, and spiritual factors can interact to cause depression, including the following:

Genetics and biochemistry. Many, if not most, cases appear linked to imbalances (for lack of a better word) in chemical messengers, known as *neurotransmitters*, within the brain. These compounds move in and out of the microscopic gaps between neurons (nerve cells) throughout the nervous system, allowing for interaction between cells in a rapid and extraordinarily complex manner. There are many different neurotransmitters, but those that are prominently linked to mood include *serotonin*, *norepinephrine*, and *dopamine*.

Disturbances in the regulation or balance of these compounds between neurons in certain areas of the brain are associated with mood disturbances. Exactly how they affect mood, why they become abnormal, and to what degree they are the cause (instead of the result) of the mood problem remain tantalizing questions. But their importance is confirmed by the dramatic effect of medications that adjust neurotransmitter levels for people with anxiety or depressive disorders.

Very often, the vulnerability to a neurotransmitter disturbance appears to have a genetic origin, such that the same type of mood disturbance will appear in multiple members and generations of the same family. This appears to be biologically driven, and not merely the result of parenting patterns or children imitating behaviors they see in a parent. It can also account for an individual becoming depressed for no apparent reason, or struggling with depression throughout life.

Personal and family events. A child who is brought up in an atmosphere of love, stability, encouragement, and consistent boundaries will usually see her world differently and interact with it more successfully than one who has lived with abuse, indifference, or chaos. For many people, depression is deeply rooted in early childhood experiences that taught them that the world is a dangerous place where no one can be trusted.

Recent stresses and reversals. One or more major losses or traumatic events can set off a depressive episode (often referred to as a *reactive depression*) that is more prolonged and profound than the normal grieving process. Examples of such stressful events are a severe illness or death of a parent or other loved one (even a pet); parental separation, divorce, or remarriage; a move from a familiar home; one or more episodes of physical or sexual abuse; a natural disaster; war or violence in the community; difficulty or failure in school or an athletic pursuit; the breakup of a close friendship or romantic relationship; or a severe or chronic illness.

Personal and family faith. A meaningful relationship with God and a sense of His love and involvement in our lives can have a significant stabilizing effect on mood and behavior. An ongoing personal commitment to God and positive connections with others who are caring and like-minded in faith serve to build a teenager's emotional world on a firm foundation, such that it will not crumble when the inevitable strains and storms of life arrive. Unfortunately, some religious situations involving intense legalism or an atmosphere of continuing condemnation can contribute to anxiety and depression.

What can be done about depression?

Depression is not a character weakness or a sign of parental failure. It is as important and *treatable* a problem as diabetes or asthma, and like those conditions, it can lead to serious consequences—including death—if it is ignored. This disorder can occur even in the most stable home where children have been reared by devoted parents who provide consistent love and limits. Remember that for many individuals depression is caused primarily by a biochemical imbalance in the brain and not by bad parenting or a personal crisis. Don't assume that "it can't happen in our home," because in doing so you might ignore or write off as a "bad attitude" significant changes in mood or behavior that desperately need your attention.

First and foremost, listen carefully to your teenager, and take her feelings and problems seriously. Expressions of worry or a sad mood should never be met with indifference or (worse) a shallow rebuff ("You'll get over it" or "Snap out of it!"). Sit down, shut off the TV, look your child in the eye, and really listen—without judging, rebuking, or trivializing it. It might help enormously if you can say honestly that you (or others you know and respect) have struggled with some of the same feelings.

Get a physician's evaluation. Usually a number of physical symptoms, such as fatigue or headaches, will need to be assessed, and rarely a specific disorder (for example, an abnormal level of thyroid hormone) will be responsible for the entire gamut of emotional and physical complaints.

Get counseling with a qualified individual about the issues of life, including past problems, family interactions, stressful situations, and other concerns. This should be carried out with someone who is trained to do this type of work with young people and who also shares your basic values. Do not assume that a depression can be "straightened out" in one or two counseling sessions. Normally, several weeks (sometimes months) of work will be necessary. Be prepared to involve yourself at some point in the process. No depression occurs in a vacuum, and family dynamics very often are part of both the problem and the solution.

Be aware of the types of input your teenager is receiving when his emotions are stormy. We've already mentioned the dark themes emanating from some corners of popular culture. If the music pounding through his headphones is feeding his brain a steady stream of rage and pessimism, a moratorium on this material would be in order. (Indeed, this would be wise even if he *isn't* depressed.)

But what about those speaking directly to him? Is he being ridiculed, bullied, or isolated at school? Are his interactions fueling self-destructive thoughts? It is possible to find *anything* on the Internet—including irresponsible individuals and websites that encourage your child or adolescent to commit suicide. Calmly but persistently talk with him, talk with his friends, and yes, even look through his room and check his computer when he's at school. Your responsibility for his life and health override any considerations of privacy.

Continue to support and pray for your depressed child. She needs to know you are there for her and that you do not think of her as crazy or a colossal failure for having this problem. Prayer serves as an acknowledgment by parent and child that God alone has a complete understanding of this complex situation. Counseling and medication may serve as useful tools, but they are best used under His guidance.

What about antidepressants?
Drug therapy can play an important role in the treatment of depression. Antidepressants can normalize disturbances in

neurotransmitter function and are neither addictive nor "an escape from reality." On the contrary, more often than not, they allow the depressed individual to tackle life issues more effectively, and they greatly accelerate the recovery process. The decision to use one or more of these medications will involve a careful discussion with a physician who is well versed in their use in children and adolescents. This will either be a psychiatrist who cares for this age-group or a primary-care physician (a pediatrician or family practitioner) who is experienced in prescribing antidepressants for young people and monitoring progress and any side effects. Assuming that positive results are obtained, it is common to continue medication on a maintenance basis for a number of months. (The neurochemistry of depression is not like a streptococcal throat infection that can be resolved with ten days of treatment.)

The most widely used antidepressants in both adults and children are called selective serotonin reuptake inhibitors (or SSRIs). Introduced in the late 1980s, this class of medication revolutionized the medical treatment of mood disorders because of markedly improved safety profiles, fewer side effects, and effectiveness for both major depression and a broad spectrum of anxiety disorders. They have also been helpful for many women with significant premenstrual distress. SSRIs currently available include fluoxetine (Prozac—the first of these on the market), sertraline (Zoloft), paroxetine (Paxil), fluvoxamine (Luvox), citalopram (Celexa), and escitalopram (Lexapro). Venlafaxine (Effexor) and duloxetine (Cymbalta) affect two neurotransmitters, serotonin and norepinephrine.

Though all of these medications have been used widely to treat depression and anxiety syndromes in adults, only fluoxetine (Prozac) has been formally approved by the Food and Drug Administration (FDA) for treating major depression in both children and adolescents, while escitalopram (Lexapro) has been approved for treating depression in adolescents twelve years and older. (Fluoxetine, sertraline, and fluvoxamine have also been approved for treating a form of chronic anxiety known as *obsessive-compulsive disorder* in this age-group.) One reason for the limited spectrum of antidepressants sanctioned by the FDA for children and adolescents is that there are far fewer controlled studies of the effects of these drugs on young people compared to those for adults. Nevertheless, experienced practitioners have successfully utilized a variety of antidepressants to treat depression in younger patients—but they also have been aware that some children and adolescents can become more irritable, anxious, or even agitated when started on these medications.

There are several reasons why some children and adolescents might feel more agitated or even suicidal when first given antidepressants:

- A small percentage of depressed adults actually have *bipolar disorder* (previously known as *manic-depressive disorder*), and when first treated with antidepressants they often feel more anxious and agitated. Among children presenting with depression for the first time, a higher percentage have bipolar disorder and may thus react unfavorably to antidepressants.
- Some who are treated for depression will feel more energetic before their sad mood lifts. But a person who is both depressed and energetic may decide to "do something"— especially an impulsive, self-destructive act.
- Some people respond to antidepressants with *akathisia*—an unpleasant sensation that one cannot hold still physically or mentally, especially when a medication is started or a dose is increased. Children may be more prone to this side effect.
- Some antidepressants are associated with unpleasant sensations, such as anxiety and irritability, when one or more

doses are missed. Fluoxetine (Prozac) has a long duration of action and is uncommonly associated with this effect.

Given these concerns, one might wonder whether anti-depressants should ever be given to children or teenagers. Though it is inappropriate to use these medications without careful evaluation and follow-up, it would also be very unwise for a parent to refuse this type of treatment for a young person who truly needs it. Antidepressants can be helpful—even lifesaving—and safe when given with appropriate precautions and proper supervision.

- Make sure both you and your teenager have a basic under-standing of what the medication is supposed to do and how it is to be taken. *Do not change or drop doses without talking with the prescribing physician.*
- You would be wise to arrange for counseling for your teen-ager while medication is being used. Talking regularly with a professional who works with young people can identify stressors, clarify issues at home and school, improve cop-ing skills, and serve as an additional safety net when the going gets tough.
- Keep checking in with your teenager about how she is feel-ing. Make sure she understands that she can and should tell you if she is having suicidal thoughts or other bother-some symptoms while taking medication.

The FDA recommends that a child or adolescent who is starting an antidepressant be followed closely by the prescribing physi-cian. It is very important that both child and parent report any side effects or changes in behavior—*especially* if these involve increas-ing anxiety or irritability—as well as any self-destructive thoughts or actions.

What about hospitalization?

In severe cases, where the emotions have been extremely unstable or there has been suicidal behavior, hospitalization may be recommended in order to initiate treatment and ensure safety. The type of program utilized will vary considerably, depending on community resources, health insurance benefits, and the needs of the depressed individual.

What are the signs of suicidal behavior?

Many of the unique features of depression among young people also increase their risk of suicide. In particular, the intensity of their emotions and a shortage of life experiences that might allow them to imagine a hopeful future beyond an immediate crisis may give rise to self-destructive behavior, especially on an impulsive basis. In order to reduce the chance of a tragic loss of life, be aware not only of the signs of depression, which have already been listed, but also of the following risks and warning signs:

- *A previous suicide attempt.* This is considered the most significant predictor of a future suicide.
- *A family history of suicide.* Compared to their non-suicidal peers, teenagers who kill themselves are more likely than their peers to have a family member who has committed suicide.
- *Expressions of intense guilt or hopelessness.*
- *Threatening, talking, or joking about suicide.* It is important to have a heart-to-heart conversation with any child or adolescent who makes comments such as "I would be better off dead" or "Nothing matters anymore." Find out what is going on in his life and how he is feeling, and make it clear that you are committed to obtaining whatever help he might need to work through his problems. Broaching the subject of suicide does not encourage it, but rather

increases the likelihood that a successful intervention can be started.

- *"Cleaning house."* You should be very concerned and should investigate immediately if a teenager—whether your own or a member of someone else's family—begins to give away clothing or other favorite possessions. This is a common behavior among young people who are planning suicide.
- *A gun in the home.* Among young people, more suicides are carried out using firearms than by any other method. If anyone in your family—especially a teenager—is having a problem with depression, remove all guns from the home and keep them out.
- *Alcohol or drug abuse.* One frightening aspect of substance abuse is that it can trigger erratic, self-destructive behavior for which little or no warning was given. A mild depression can suddenly plummet to suicidal intensity with the help of drugs or alcohol. Because of the unpredictable actions of chemicals on the system, a number of deaths occur among teenagers who did not intend to hurt themselves.
- *Suicide among other adolescents in your community.* Occasionally one or more suicides in a community or school precipitate a disastrous "cluster" of self-destructive behavior among local teens.
- *A sudden, major loss or humiliation.* All of the stressful life events that were listed earlier in this chapter—such as the death of a loved one, parental separation, or failure on an important test—can not only provoke a depressive episode but also precipitate an unexpected suicide attempt.

If you believe there is any possibility of a self-destructive act by your child, it is important that you not only express your concern, but also *seek help immediately*. You may want to contact your teen's physician for advice or referral. If anyone in your family has dealt with a counselor, this individual may be the appropriate initial contact. An evaluation at the nearest emergency department may be necessary. Many communities have a mental-health center that offers on-the-spot assessment of an individual's suicide risk. Some even have an assessment team that will come to your home. *Stay with your teen* (or make certain that he or she remains in the company of a responsible adult) until you have reasonable assurance from a qualified individual and a clear commitment from your son or daughter that suicide is not going to be attempted. In situations where assurance cannot be obtained, the suicidal individual may need to be hospitalized for safety, further assessment, and the initiation of treatment. You will also need to take appropriate safety precautions, including removing any guns from the home and controlling access to medications.

What do I do if my child attempts suicide?

Fortunately, the vast majority of suicide attempts by teens are unsuccessful. Some of these result in significant medical problems, while many are considered gestures or cries for help. *Any deliberate self-destructive act, whether planned or impulsive, should be taken very seriously, regardless of the severity of the outcome.* An evaluation at an emergency room should be carried out; subsequent hospitalization for medical treatment or observation is not uncommon.

After any medical problems have been resolved, a formal assessment by a qualified professional is mandatory. The course of action to be taken will depend on a number of factors and may range from ongoing counseling while your teen remains at home to a formal treatment program in a psychiatric hospital setting. The latter approach is usually chosen both to ensure safety and to begin intensive treatment. Though the details of treatment that might be used in such settings are beyond the scope of this book, it is important that you understand and approve of the approaches that will be used with your teenager and play an active role in her recovery process. As upset or guilty as you might feel under such circumstances, this is the time to draw close to your child and not to communicate shock or dismay ("How could you do such a thing?"). Above all, she will need loving and optimistic people on her team, and it will help immensely if her parents are at the top of the list.

CHAPTER 7

PREPARING TO PASS THE BATON

Train a child in the way he should go,
and when he is old he will not turn from it.

PROVERBS 22:6

As a PARENT, you have been entrusted by God to help mold your teenager's character, values, and spirituality while preparing her for such practical matters as choosing a career, handling finances, and finding a spouse. This is a tall order, but the important assignment of preparing adolescents for the future can indeed be accomplished—one small step at a time.

How can I set goals for this process?

The first step is to define what your specific goals should be. This chapter is intended to help by serving as a basic road map, one that can be reviewed every year to gauge whether your race is still on course and the baton ready to be passed. You may find the length and breadth of this endeavor daunting. *How can I instill my values and virtues in my children? I'm still trying to develop them in my own life!* If you realize you can't accomplish all of these goals perfectly and that you can't be an infallible guide to life for your child (because you're still figuring out a few things yourself), congratulations! Acknowledging this fact is the beginning of parental wisdom. You can be certain that God knew your shortcomings before entrusting you with a child, and you would be wise to seek His counsel on a regular basis.

As you think about these concepts, you may experience misgivings or even remorse. You probably haven't cherished every moment with your child (few parents do), and it's likely that at some point (if not many times) you may have felt burdened with—or even resentful of—the demands of parenting. Perhaps your child is in the midst of a stormy adolescence and you are painfully aware that you have not exactly been the world's best cheerleader, teacher, or coach. But it is never too late to make course corrections—and amends—as a parent. Even after your children are fully grown, what you have learned (sometimes the hard way) can still benefit *their* children. What ultimately matters is that you ask for forgiveness where it is needed and then move forward, providing input and support that is appropriate for their current stage of life.

How can I nuture my teenager's faith in God?

Sadly, some children who have regularly attended Sunday school and church will grow up to ignore God and reject the values their parents taught (or *thought* they had taught) at home. To their utter dismay, Mom and Dad learn too late that this training just didn't "take," and they wonder what went wrong.

A child's acquisition of spiritual values encompasses far more than learning some Bible stories, singing songs about Jesus, or bowing his head for a few moments before taking the first bite of dinner, as meaningful as these activities might be. Indeed, the transmission of spiritual values cannot and should not be isolated from the overall task of shaping your child's character—an assignment that begins during the toddler years and isn't concluded until he is launched into independent adulthood. If what you communicate about a relationship with God doesn't affect behavior, develop character, and bring about moral and mental improvement, it is little more than sanctified hot air.

Do you have a clear understanding of your beliefs about God and your relationship with Him? While many mothers and fathers have spent years cultivating a living, growing, and well-articulated faith, others arrive at parenthood with little or no sense of God's role in their lives, except perhaps for some religious teachings and experiences dimly remembered from childhood. Some sense that their children should go to Sunday school or receive some type of religious training, even if they themselves don't buy into those teachings. If you are in the latter category, we would highly recommend Tim Keller's book *The Reason for God* (Dutton, 2008) as an intelligent and gracious orientation to the teachings of the Bible about our relationship to God.

The plot thickens when Mom and Dad are not on the same page, or even in the same book, spiritually speaking: What should the kids be taught, and by whom? Obviously, the more unified parents are on this important subject, and the earlier these questions are addressed, the better—but it's never too late. Regular communication with your spouse about your individual and mutual spiritual journeys isn't just for Sunday morning; it's a vital topic for everyday conversation. If you are a single parent or are married to someone who is disinterested in this subject, by all means find a pastor, mature friend, or counselor who is willing to talk with you about it.

What effect does prayer have on my teenager's spiritual growth?

Prayer is the most important component of the whole process of transmitting spiritual values to our teens (not to mention the rest of our parenting responsibilities). One of the biggest mistakes we could make is to assume we can "dial in" a teenager's decision to commit her life to Jesus Christ and serve Him wholeheartedly. Acknowledging our lack of control over our child's physical and spiritual future, and our dependence on the One who holds it, is the beginning of wisdom. Find a time or occasion every day— perhaps as you are rising in the morning or settling in for a night's sleep—to bring your child before God in prayer and to be transparent with Him about your joys and concerns for this young life He has entrusted to you.

How much of a role do family issues play in my teenager's growth?

What kind of emotional attraction—or baggage—does your everyday family life attach to your spiritual values? Is your home a place where love, safety, sanity, good humor, kindness, and appropriate limits are continually in residence? Or is it a place where anger, arguments, chaos, bitterness, and extremes of discipline (whether authoritarian or permissive) are the (dis)order of the day? Obviously, no family is perfect, but keep in mind that the soil of the young heart in which you sow spiritual seeds will be strongly affected by the prevailing emotional climate at home. Many prodigals who spend months or years wandering away from God during adolescence or young adulthood are drawn back toward the faith they were taught during childhood because of their emotional ties to family and home. Sadly, too many would-be disciples have become long-term prodigals because they were desperate to escape a painful home environment that included a lot of empty, or even toxic, religious talk.

Are you aware of the impact of your own childhood experiences on your approach to spiritual matters in your home? If family devotions were the low point of your week (for whatever reason) as a child, you may mistakenly assume they can't be successful with your own children. If your parents were noncommittal or disinterested in spiritual matters, you might find yourself gravitating to the opposite extreme of trying to micromanage your child's faith. Or if your spiritual upbringing was steeped in legalism that emphasized "rules and regs" rather than a loving relationship with God, you may be tempted to take a hands-off approach that assumes your kids can figure out their faith without your input.

Every family is a unique civilization with its own history, traditions, and patterns of everyday living—including the ways in which God is discussed and honored. The spiritual traditions with which you grew up may serve as a wonderful foundation for your family to build upon, or they may include baggage you want to throw overboard so that you can start fresh with your own children.

An excellent resource for parents who are concerned about the viability and vitality of faith that their teen carries into adulthood is the book *Sticky Faith* by Kara E. Powell and Chap Clark (Zondervan, 2011). This book and the website associated with it—http://stickyfaith.org—contain a wealth of intelligent and useful insights on this critical topic for both parents and youth group leaders.

How should I handle tough questions?

Your teenager should be learning the reasons and rationale behind your rules as well as internalizing your values. If your middle-schooler asks why it's wrong to have sex outside of marriage, helping her understand a sound, biblical perspective will provide the conviction for her to make wise decisions about sexuality. Similarly, if she asks some probing questions about God, the Bible, or troubling events—"Why would God allow so many people to die in that earthquake last week?"—avoid giving pat answers or shutting down the conversation because you're not comfortable with the direction it seems to be going. Having strong convictions and a solid grasp of Scripture doesn't mean that complex issues must be reduced to simplistic formulas, or that you must have the answer to everything, or that you can't have some respectful and productive dialogue with someone whose beliefs don't exactly match your own—especially when that person is your child.

How can I help my teenager develop character?

The development of positive, stable character traits should flow directly from spiritual growth. If a teenager's religious activities and affirmations don't have any consistent impact on his behavior, then his faith is shallow, false, or self-deluding (see James 2:14-17).

Similarly, attempts to train a child to be "good" will have only limited success if he or she does not have an understanding of God's love and justice, the need for genuine repentance, and the importance of ongoing submission to God's leadership. A teenager can make all the right spiritual noises and toe the line when her parents are watching—but what happens when no one is looking, or when she's tempted to compromise?

Spiritual maturity and virtuous character traits that will continue into adulthood will not develop during random lectures crammed into a few minutes every month. You'll need to plan ahead, focusing on the values you intend to instill. You can also take advantage of unscheduled "teachable moments," when a situation naturally lends itself to a discussion about positive (or negative) behavior. However this important task is carried out, the following are some important character traits, listed alphabetically, on which to focus.

Courage is frequently portrayed in movies and cartoons as the primary requirement for superheroes embroiled in daring exploits. But teenagers need to understand that courage is also important for everyday life, both now and in the future. Indeed, one who learns courage as a child is more likely to be secure as an adult. Courage encompasses several elements:

- daring to attempt difficult but worthy projects
- saying no to the pressure of the crowd
- remaining true to one's convictions, even when they are unpopular or inconvenient
- being outgoing and friendly, even when it's uncomfortable

Courage can also apply to more stressful situations:

- applying resources in creative ways when faced with overwhelming odds
- following difficult instructions in the face of danger
- confronting an opponent in an honorable way, confident that what is morally right will ultimately succeed

Determination can help your teenager avoid becoming a pessimist. This trait will help him

- realize that present struggles are essential for future achievement;
- break down a seemingly impossible task by concentrating on achievable goals;
- expend whatever energy is necessary to complete a project;
- reject any distraction that will hinder the completion of a task; and
- prepare to handle hardships that lie ahead, whether the task is spiritual, physical, emotional, or relational.

Fidelity and chastity are rarely taught in today's culture (by movies, television programs, popular music, etc.) or by educators, coaches, or even church leaders. Therefore, it is important that your teenager hear clearly from you about the benefits of reserving sexual activity for marriage. Teens also need to grasp the serious potential consequences of sexual immorality: sexually transmitted infections and diseases, infertility, crisis pregnancies, and broken hearts.

Honesty is not always rewarded in our culture, but it is a bedrock virtue. Without it, your teen's most important relationships will be compromised and unstable. Teenagers should be taught that truthfulness is critical when dealing with family members, friends and acquaintances, school, organizations (including future employers), governmental agencies, and God. Dishonesty must be discouraged in all its forms, whether it be outright lying to another individual, misrepresenting to an employer what one has (or hasn't) done, cheating on a test, plagiarizing, or doctoring an income tax return.

Humility arises from an honest assessment of one's own strengths and weaknesses, such that boasting is not necessary to gain acceptance or to feel contentment. Humility also involves submission to duly constituted authority, obedience to the law, and fairness in work and play. Most important, humility will keep your teenager on her knees in prayer.

Kindness and friendliness should be presented as admirable and far superior to being "tough." Teenagers need to be taught that it is usually better to understand than to confront, and that gentleness—especially toward those who are younger or weaker—is in fact a sign of strength. *Do not allow your teenager to become a bully.*

Love in many ways encompasses and surpasses other virtues (see 1 Corinthians 13:4-7). Teenagers should be taught—and shown—how to love their friends, neighbors, and even adversaries.

Loyalty and dependability are traits needed for success in many arenas of life. A person who is flighty and cannot honor a commitment is unlikely to find true happiness or success. Your teenager needs to learn the importance of loyalty to family, employer, country, church, school, and other organizations and institutions to which he will eventually make commitments. If a teenager learns to be reliable and stand by his word, he will be trusted and see opportunities open before him throughout life.

Orderliness and cleanliness may or may not be "next to godliness," but they can increase a person's chances of success in many areas of life. Though no one has ever died of dirty-room syndrome, a teenager who can learn to keep her possessions organized will eventually be able to use her resources to their greatest efficiency. Personal cleanliness and good grooming speak of self-respect and project an important message to others.

Respect is a critical commodity in human relationships, whether within families, organizations, or entire nations. It has largely been lost in our culture, and it desperately needs to be regained. Respect encompasses basic courtesy, politeness, and manners toward others—and much more. While teenagers should receive basic training in polite speech and manners, these can also be a facade that masks contempt for the other person. True respect encompasses not only speech, but also core attitudes and behavior toward virtually everything—life, property, parents, those in proper authority, friends, strangers, the beliefs and rights of others, nature, and—most of all—God.

While disrespectful behavior may reflect ignorance, or at worst selfish and destructive attitudes, too many teenagers have lost respect for their own bodies and minds long before they arrive at adulthood. Though parents want (and should receive) respect from their children, they must also remember that respect in all of its dimensions should be modeled every day at home.

Self-discipline and moderation are rare but valuable traits in a culture that claims that you can—and should—have it all. Teenagers need to understand that, even if it is possible for them to do so, it is not necessary or wise to "have it all." Exercising self-discipline over physical, emotional, and financial desires can prevent illness, debt, and burnout later in life. They should be taught the importance of the following values:

- controlling personal appetites
- knowing the limits of body and mind
- balancing work and recreation
- avoiding the dangers of extreme, unbalanced viewpoints
- engaging the brain before putting the tongue in gear

Unselfishness and sensitivity are universally appreciated and respected. Teenagers who are more concerned about others than themselves will be seen as mature beyond their years and can benefit themselves and others.

How do I help my teenager manage money?

Teaching children how to manage money can be one of the greatest benefits parents provide for them before they leave home. Before you attempt to teach your teen about money, however, determine how you are doing with your own finances.

Do you set goals? Are you out of debt? Do you have long-term and short-term savings? Have you begun investing in a college-education fund or saving for your retirement? If so, you're definitely making wise decisions. On the other hand, do you live from paycheck to paycheck? Do you have trouble keeping track of how much money is in your checking account? Is there always "too much month at the end of the money"? Are you an impulse buyer? Do you depend on your credit cards to make ends meet? If this is the case, before you start teaching your child how to manage money, you need to get your own spending habits in order.

Whether you are a financial wizard or still struggling to balance your checkbook, the most important lesson your teenager needs to learn about money is that *God owns it all*. God is the creator and ultimate owner of every resource, and He has entrusted you to be a wise steward of whatever He has loaned to you.

It is important to realize that children begin shaping their views about money at an early age. Unfortunately, many families deal with this important topic haphazardly, offering their children little specific guidance while presuming they can learn the nuts and bolts of money management when they're older. But if you wait until your kids are ready to leave the nest before you begin to broach this subject, they may enter adulthood at a serious disadvantage when it comes to handling their finances wisely.

As a starting point, formulate coherent policies within your family for the following issues. Keep in mind that there are several possible approaches and reasonable viewpoints for each issue.

Unpaid responsibilities. Every teenager should have certain jobs at home to do regularly without any specific pay. These might involve tasks related to their own possessions (e.g., keeping a clean bedroom and doing laundry), as well as chores done for the good of the entire family (setting the table or feeding the dog). Teenagers should know that it is usual and customary for everyone in the family to pitch in and work for the common good without expecting a reward every time.

Budgeting. This will be important whether your teenager's future income is modest or abundant. Beginning at sixteen or seventeen, your adolescent should be allowed to make most of her own financial decisions. You may choose to provide her with a monthly allowance to be budgeted among several items such as clothing, toiletries, and other personal supplies you used to buy. Help her set up a budget, but she must also be given the freedom to fail—and in the process learn valuable lessons. For example, if she blows her entire clothing budget in the first six months of the year, she will have to forgo desirable purchases later on. Allocating cash between basic necessities, entertainment, savings, and giving to church and other worthy causes is a concept most teens do not understand without some guidance. But if you teach your teenager budgeting principles now, she'll benefit for a lifetime.

Managing a checking account. Your adolescent should be given the opportunity to use and maintain his own checking account under your supervision. It is vitally important that you teach an older teenager how to balance a checkbook monthly. Many parents obtain a credit card (with a very modest spending limit) for an older child—perhaps in the senior year of high school—to train him to use it properly. Make sure your teenager understands two foundational principles for credit or debit card use: (1) Never buy anything with a card that he would not have purchased with cash, and (2) pay off the total amount on the credit card each month without fail.

Personal expenses: Spending and bargain hunting. Your adolescent, whether living at home or away at college, should begin to understand how "miscellaneous expenses" can derail a budget. Teach her to use self-control in her spending through your example. Show her where to shop and help her learn to seek the best values for her limited supply of dollars.

How do I prepare my teenager for a career?
Children begin thinking about "what I want to be when I grow up" early in life, as they play with their friends and watch their parent(s) go off to work every day. An ideal time to start career preparation is during the preteen years. Take the time to expose

your children to a variety of occupations. If your daughter is interested in medicine, for example, let her spend time talking to her physician about the demands and rewards of this profession. The same approach can be taken for virtually any type of career that might interest your child.

Guiding and equipping your adolescent with the skills needed to be gainfully employed is a major responsibility, one that must begin before he leaves home. The following are some ideas that might help in this process.

Equip your adolescent to discover her strengths and weaknesses.

- Expose your teenager to job opportunities that fit her personality.
- Don't project your expectations on your child. Not all children follow in their parents' footsteps. If you're an accountant but your teen has difficulty with math, don't push her into a career that would make her miserable. If you're an attorney but your daughter wants to be an artist, don't try to make her fit her artistic "square peg" temperament into the "round hole" demands of a legal career.
- Help your teen discover her natural, God-given talents. During your child's formative years, she will excel in some areas and fail at others. Help her develop her strengths and identify possible career opportunities that might match them.

Equip your adolescent to think of vocation and career in spiritual terms.

- He is uniquely designed by God (see Psalm 139:13-14).
- He has been given specific talents for a purpose (see Romans 12:6-8).

- He must develop his God-given talents and strive for excellence (see Proverbs 22:29).
- Work is a stage for his higher calling (see Matthew 5:16).

Equip your adolescent to obtain guidance in the pursuit of education, training, and possible career fields.
You should be able to get some help in this area from her high school's professional guidance counselor.

- Identify your adolescent's likes and dislikes and expose her to fields she is interested in.
- Discover natural talents before college or vocational training. Work with your teen (for example, by becoming involved with her in her science class). Before spending thousands of dollars on college or vocational training, help your teenager find the path on which she is most likely to excel.
- Teach your teenager to pray for God's guidance and seek what He would have her do for a career.

Finally, consider seeking career-testing services online that may help your teenager determine what career options best fit his personality. These tests often help young adults hone in on their special talents, if they have not already done so, and they can also confirm whether a certain career choice is a logical path. Adolescents who are somewhat aimless might find that the test results point them in one or more specific directions. Others who are endowed with a number of definite interests might benefit from tests that help them focus on their areas of greatest strength. This might spare at least some from changing majors one or more times during college, which could prove both expensive and time-consuming.

How do I begin to prepare my teenager for marriage?

One of our most important goals as parents when passing the baton to our children is to prepare them for marriage. Although not every child will grow up to marry, many will. If you have a strong and vibrant marriage, it is important to share with your child the principles on which you have built and maintained this relationship. But if your marriage is less than ideal or you have experienced a divorce, lessons you have learned the hard way can still benefit your teenager, assuming you are willing to be candid and transparent about your experience.

At a time when more than 40 percent of marriages will end in divorce, parents face a formidable job educating their children about selecting a husband or a wife for life. Because we are a mobile society, children from stable and loving homes often select partners with different backgrounds, customs, goals, interests, and beliefs. This does not mean they cannot succeed in marriage, but in such cases both parties must enter the relationship with their eyes open and a willingness to work through their differences.

Early adolescence is a good time to begin discussing with your children characteristics and traits to seek in a future wife or husband. You may want to give them a list of twenty or thirty of these qualities and have them rank in order the ones they think are the most important. Quite often, children will discover that their mental image of their "dream partner"—frequently a fantasy derived from movies and television shows—does not match with this ranking. It might be helpful to have your teenager save this list (or make a copy) and review it annually.

Also, early in adolescence—perhaps on a special birthday such as the thirteenth—encourage your teen to begin praying for her future spouse. As a parent, you should be doing the same if you haven't started already. Toward the end of high school, give your adolescent some books that explore the process of selecting a partner and building a strong marriage. You would be wise to read them yourself and set aside some time to discuss them with your teenager.

Inform your teenager that, even when married, he will need to work on the marriage relationship for a lifetime.

Finally, *warn your teenager once more about becoming sexually involved before marriage.* Among other things, premarital sex might lead him to marry the wrong person and rob them of a satisfying, lifelong marriage. Children of divorce might be tempted to cohabit prior to marriage in hopes of avoiding their parents' mistakes. But statistics from a variety of sources indicate that cohabitants have a greater chance of divorce than those who wait until marriage to live together. An excellent resource that explores the downside of moving in without marrying is Glenn Stanton's book *The Ring Makes All the Difference: The Hidden Consequences of Cohabitation and the Strong Benefits of Marriage* (Moody Publishers, 2011).

The most important thing you can do for teenagers to help them develop a healthy concept of marriage is to allow them to see you loving, cherishing, and respecting your partner. If you are not married, allow your children to spend time with one or more families in which a nurturing, respectful marital relationship is modeled.

When is my parenting job finished?

In reality, you have been slowly releasing your child since birth. There will come a time when you must pass the baton to your child. Of course, you will be a parent for life, but your role must change to that of a coach and friend, encouraging your grown child's progress—and perhaps later on watching your grandchildren take the baton to begin their lap.

Notes

1. R. Schellenberg, "Treatment for the Premenstrual Syndrome with Agnus Castus Fruit Extract: Prospective, Randomised, Placebo Controlled Study," *BMJ* 2001; 322 (7279):134, http://www.uptodate.com/contents/treatment-of-premenstrual-syndrome-and-premenstrual-dysphoric-disorder/abstract/58?utdPopup=true.
2. Multiple studies are referenced in the online resource *UpToDate* at http://www.uptodate.com/contents/treatment-of-premenstrual-syndrome-and-premenstrual-dysphoric-disorder?source=search_result&search=premenstrual+syndrome&selectedTitle=1%7E150. Research studies will usually compare what happens when one group of subjects takes a drug, herb, or other treatment while a similar group takes a *placebo*, a substance formulated to have no effect whatsoever.
3. W. Cates Jr, "Estimates of the Incidence and Prevalence of Sexually Transmitted Diseases in the United States," American Social Health Association Panel, *Sexually Transmitted Diseases*, 1999; 26 (4:Suppl):S2–S7.
4. L. A. Koutsky and N. B. Kiviat, "Genital Human Papillomavirus," in K. K. Holmes, P. A. Mardh, P. F. Sparling, et al., eds. *Sexually Transmitted Diseases*. 3rd ed. (New York: McGraw-Hill, 1999), 347–359.
5. J. M. Walboomers, M. V. Jacobs, M. M. Manos, et al. "Human Papillomavirus Is a Necessary Cause of Invasive Cervical Cancer Worldwide," *J Pathology*, 189 (1999):12–19.
6. Robert I Haddad, "Human Papillomavirus-Associated Head and Neck Cancer." Last literature review version 19.2: *UpToDate*: May 2011. This topic last updated: March 24, 2011. http://www.uptodate.com/contents/human-papillomavirus-associated-head-and-neck-cancer/abstract/6-9.

7. American Cancer Society, "What Are the Key Statistics about Cervical Cancer?" http://www.cancer.org/Cancer/CervicalCancer/DetailedGuide /cervical-cancer-key-statistics, accessed 9-22-11.

8. American Cancer Society, "What Are the Key Statistics about Oral Cavity and Oropharyngeal Cancers?" http://www.cancer.org/Cancer/OralCavity andOropharyngealCancer/DetailedGuide/oral-cavity-and-oropharyngeal -cancer-key-statistics, accessed 9-21-11.

9. Amanda Lenhart, Rich Ling, Scott Campbell, et al., "Teens and Mobile Phones," Pew Research Center, April 20, 2010; http://www.pewinternet .org/Reports/2010/Teens-and-Mobile-Phones.aspx.

10. K. Perper, K. Peterson, and J. Manlove, *Diploma Attachment among Teen Mothers*, 2010 Child Trends, Fact Sheet: Washington, D.C. Retrieved March 2010 from http://www.childtrends.org/Files//Child_Trends-2010 _01_22_FS_DiplomaAttainment.pdf. Cited in "Teen Pregnancy and Education," The National Campaign to Prevent Teen Pregnancy, March 2010, http://www.thenationalcampaign.org/why-it-matters/pdf /education.pdf, accessed 12-5-11.

11. See http://www.cdc.gov/tobacco/data_statistics/fact_sheets/youth_data /tobacco_use/index.htm.

12. See http://www.cdc.gov/mmwr/preview/mmwrhtml/mm5933a2.htm.

13. Substance Abuse and Mental Health Services Administration (2008). Results from the 2008 National Survey on Drug Use and Health Office of Applied Studies, NSDUH Series H-36, DHHS Publication No. SMA 09-4434. Referenced in "Children and Teens," American Lung Association, http://www.lungusa.org/stop-smoking/about-smoking /facts-figures/children-teens-and-tobacco.html, accessed 1-11-12.

14. American Lung Association, February 2010, http://www.lungusa.org /stop-smoking/about-smoking/facts-figures/children-teens-and-tobacco .html.

15. See the Substance Abuse and Mental Health Service's (SAMHSA) 2010 National Survey on Drug Use and Health: http://www.samhsa.gov/data /NSDUH/2k10Results/Web/PDFW/2k10Results.pdf.

16. As of 2010, OcyContin tablets have been reformulated to make them more difficult (though not impossible) to manipulate for "recreational" (abusive) purposes.

17. Centers for Disease Control, "HIV Incidence," http://www.cdc.gov /hiv/topics/surveillance/incidence.htm; "Hepatitis C FAQs for Health Professionals," http://www.cdc.gov/hepatitis/hcv/hcvfaq.htm.

18. See http://www.stopbullying.gov/topics/what_is_bullying/index.html. StopBullying.gov is an online resource managed by the Department of Health & Human Services in partnership with the Department of Education and the Department of Justice.

19. Youth Risk Behavior Surveillance—United States, 2009. Centers for Disease Control Morbidity and Mortality Weekly Report, June 4, 2010, Volume 59, No. SS-5, http://www.cdc.gov/mmwr/pdf/ss/ss5905.pdf. This is the most recent YRBS report as of the publication of this book.

20. This chapter addresses eating disorders, specifically anorexia and bulimia, in teenagers. The problem of excessive weight in adolescents is no less important, and is explored in detail in another book in this series, the *Busy Mom's Guide to Family Nutrition* (Tyndale House Publishers, 2012).

21. See http://www.cdc.gov/nchs/data/nvsr/nvsr59/nvsr59_08.pdf and http://www.mentalhealthamerica.net/index.cfm?objectid=C7DF950F -1372-4D20-C8B5BD8DFDD94CF1).

●●●Index

About the Author

DR. PAUL REISSER is a family physician in Southern California. He has been a member of Focus on the Family's Physicians Resource Council since 1991, and he served as the primary author of Focus on the Family's *Complete Guide to Baby and Child Care*. He married Teri, a marriage and family therapist, in 1975 and is still very happy about that decision. They have two grown children, three wonderful grandchildren, and one lovable but spoiled dog.

Look for these additional parenting resources wherever fine books are sold:

Complete Guide to Baby & Child Care is a comprehensive guidebook to parenting from before birth through the end of the teen years. It takes a balanced, commonsense approach to raising children to be healthy emotionally, physically, mentally, and spiritually. This indispensable guide delivers practical and critical information parents need to know, including 25 Special Concerns sections that cover topics such as fever in small children, effective discipline, ADHD, cyberspace safety, and much more!

Creative Correction
Drawing from her own family's experiences and from interaction with other parents, Lisa Whelchel offers creative solutions for parents who are out of ideas and desperate for new, proven approaches to discipline. In addition to advice on topics such as sibling conflict and lying, Whelchel offers a biblical perspective and down-to-earth encouragement for parents who are feeling overwhelmed.

Essentials of Parenting
Becoming a parent is one of God's greatest gifts in life. Children don't, however, come with an instruction manual, so where can parents turn to get the answers they need? Essentials of Parenting™ DVD series brings top childrearing experts into your home or church—with practical wisdom, honest confessions, and decades of experience.

Look for these additional parenting resources wherever fine books are sold:

Busy Mom's Guide to Parenting Young Children
Using a question-and-answer format, *Busy Mom's Guide to Parenting Young Children* takes you from birth through age 4 with tips on sleep patterns, potty training, developmental milestones, and more. Tired already? Get energized and equipped for the journey with this quick reference guide, and look forward to the joy of growing with your child.
(Some content previously published in the *Complete Guide to Baby & Child Care.*)

Busy Mom's Guide to Parenting Teens
Using a question-and-answer format, *Busy Mom's Guide to Parenting Teens* gives you tips and solid advice as your child heads into the teen years and develops independence. Driving, cell phones, social networking, physical and emotional changes—your teen is being bombarded with new experiences! Don't just survive your child's leap into adolescence, take the journey together and learn to thrive. Your road map is inside this book—enjoy the ride!
(Some content previously published in the *Complete Guide to Baby & Child Care.*)

Busy Mom's Guide to Family Nutrition
Using a question-and-answer format, *Busy Mom's Guide to Family Nutrition* provides bite-size pieces of information, including nutritional basics, the skinny on fats, interpreting food labels, exploring popular diet plans, and much more. Improve your family's health quotient with this quick reference guide, and enjoy your healthy family!
(Some content previously published in the *Complete Guide to Family Health, Nutrition & Fitness.*)